3

Writing and Grammar
for Key Stage 3 Tests

The **Language** Kit

John Seely

Heinemann

Heinemann Educational Publishers
Halley Court, Jordan Hill, Oxford OX2 8EJ
A division of Reed Educational and Professional Publishing Ltd

OXFORD MELBOURNE AUCKLAND
JOHANNESBURG BLANTYRE GABORONE
IBADAN PORTSMOUTH (NH) USA CHICAGO

04 03 02 01 00
10 9 8 7 6 5 4 3 2 1

ISBN 0 435 10201 X

Designed and produced by Ken Vail Graphic Design
Cover design by I E Design
Cover illustration by Anthony Rule
Illustrated by Mark Bergin, Eikon Ltd (Gerry Ball and Robert Calow),
Graham-Cameron Illustration (Michelle Ives and Brian Lee), BL Kearley Ltd
(Shirley Bellwood and Barry Wilkinson), Pantelis Palios, Tony Randell,
Linda Rogers Associates (Trevor Parkin), Elizabeth Roy Literary Agency
(Mike Phillips) and Robin Turner.
Original illustrations © Heinemann Educational Publishers 2000

Printed and bound in Spain by Edelvives

Contents

A message for teachers

Writing and Grammar for Key Stage 3 Tests has two purposes:

◆ to continue the work on writing and grammar developed in *The Language Kit* Books 1 and 2

◆ to prepare students for the Writing requirements of the Key Stage 3 Tests, using the principles and practice that are common to all three books in the series.

There is also a *Teacher's File*, which contains guidance for the teacher and the answers to the Language Skills practice items. It also gives advice and teaching materials to help use the student book in the development of reading skills for the tests.

The Student Book contains three types of unit:

◆ **Writing Skills units**
◆ **Language Skills units**
◆ **Test Practice units.**

Writing Skills units

These 11 units begin with the general principles of writing (audience, purpose, paragraphing). They then move on to the main modes of writing: narrative, description, explanation and argument. The last four units focus on key writing formats: letter, report, leaflet and article. All units are carefully cross-referenced to the relevant Language Skills units.

The approach in all the Writing Skills units is to set out the principles involved by leading students to observe them in practice, both by giving examples from real texts and by giving short practical exercises. Each unit culminates in the construction of a complete longer text, and contains guidelines for the writer. In this way all the main demands of the Key Stage 3 Tests are covered in detail.

Language Skills units

These combine reference material and short practice exercises. They can be used for class teaching or individual study. The topics covered are:

◆ vocabulary
◆ spelling
◆ word classes
◆ phrases
◆ parts of a sentence
◆ multiple sentences
◆ punctuation.

Test Practice units

These four units follow the general pattern of the Writing part of the Key Stage 3 Tests. The *Teacher's File* contains questions to cover the Reading part of the tests.

If you have any comments on these materials and suggestions for their improvement, I should be most grateful to hear from you. You can email me at: languagekit@yourenglish.com or visit my website www.yourenglish.com

Acknowledgements

The Author and Publishers should like to thank the following for permission to use copyright material:

The Orangina brand owner and A.G. Barr plc, 136 Gallowgate, Glasgow, for the 'Orangina' advertisement, p14; Consumer Surveys Ltd for part of a Questionnaire, p15; Random House UK Ltd for the cover of *The Smelly Sock Joke Book* by Susan Abbott (Red Fox Children's Books), p15; Walker Books Ltd for an extract from *Ordinary Seaman* by John Gordon, (c) 1992 John Gordon, p24; Penguin Books (Australia) Ltd for extracts from *Thirteen Unpredictable Tales*, p28 and *Uncanny* by Paul Jennings, pp30 and 115; British Telecommunications for the 'Emergency' instructions in phone books, p39; Dorling Kindersley Ltd for the extract 'Saving Lives' in *Eyewitness Guides: Future* by Michael Tambini, p39; NSPCC for the 'Full Stop' Campaign letter, p49; Mirror Syndication International for extracts from articles 'Let's get a life' by Lindsay Sutton, p56, and 'Light up winter with bulbs' by Adrienne Wild p72 in *Sunday Mirror*, 12/9/99, and 'Men and Women' by Virginia Ironside, p72 in *Sunday Mirror Magazine*, 12/9/99; The Editor, St. Helen's Star Newspaper for a news item from their website, p60; The Environment Agency for the front cover of a 'Flood Warning' leaflet, p65; The Controller of HMSO for the front covers of leaflets, p65; *Personal Computer World* for a page from the October, 1999, edition of the Magazine, p72; Brooklands Communications Ltd for pages from *The Renault Magazine* (c) Renault UK Ltd, p72; Scholastic Ltd for extracts from *Coping With Boys*, p102 and *Coping With Girls*, pp104 and 106, by Peter Corey and Kara May, and an extract from *Luce's Big Mistake* by Ann Bryant, p125; Kingfisher Publications for extracts from *Planet Earth* by Martyn Bramwell, pp110 and 113; John Gordon for extracts from his stories *The House on the Brink*, pp120, 122 and 124 and *The Dress Shop* p137; Transworld Publishers for extracts from *Hydra* by Robert Swindells, pp132 and 140, (c) Robert Swindells (Doubleday); Sheil Land Associates Ltd on behalf of Melvyn Bragg for an extract from *Speak for England* p132, (Secker & Warburg); Aidan Chambers for an extract from his story *The Kissing Game,* p135; Heinemann Education for extracts from *Class Acts* by Frank Brennan, pp136 and 138; Hodder & Stoughton Ltd for an extract from *Inventors* by Jack Marlowe, p139; Channel 4 Books and Darlow Smithson Productions for an extract from *Crash* by Nicholas Faith, p140; RSPCA for an advertisement from their website, p144; National Geographic Society for a map of Mount Everest, p146; Vegetarian Society of the United Kingdom for an advertisement from their website, pp151 and 152; The Observer Newspaper for an extract from *Life*, Nov/Dec 1997 p153; Rough Guides Ltd for extracts from *The Rough Guide to the USA*, 4th Edition, p156; Abner Stein Literary Agency on behalf of James Lee Burke for an extract from *Heaven's Prisoners*, p157.

Whilst every effort has been made to locate the owners of copyright, in some cases this has been unsuccessful. The publishers apologise for any omission of original sources and will be pleased to make the necessary arrangements at the first opportunity.

The Publishers should like to thank the following for permission to reproduce photographs on the pages noted.

Zefa/StockMarket pp32 and 35; PhotoDisc p36; Robert Harding Picture Library p36; John Seely all photos on p67; Oxford Scientific Films/Stan Osolinski p75; PhotoDisc p142.

Thinking about your audience

It is important to remember that you write to get a message across to someone –
to *communicate with your audience*. If you don't think carefully about your
audience then you won't communicate very effectively. In this unit you will be
looking at how to tell the same story to a number of different audiences.

An experiment

Imagine that you are the girl in the pictures. Think about how you would
describe what happened to you:

◆ to a friend of your own age

◆ to an adult member of your family

◆ to a police officer.

In what ways would these three versions be different? Why would they be
different?

Thinking about your audience

The main part of this unit is based on a true story. It is told in the pictures on this page and the next. Look carefully at the picture story and make sure that you understand clearly what happened.
Then turn to page 10.

The fire brigade arrived very promptly. The horse was in no danger. I am glad to say that both the young lady and the horse are perfectly all right.

Thinking about your audience

What does the reader need?

When you think about your audience, there are three questions to ask yourself:

1. How easily can they read and understand what I am writing?

2. How much do they know about this subject?

3. How well do I know them?

Reading and understanding

As you know from your own experience, some people are better readers than others. If you know that the people you are writing for are slow or inexperienced readers, then you must allow for this as you write.

1. Suppose you had to tell a small child what happened to the horse in the story. How would you begin the story? Write the first four sentences of the story you would tell.

2. Now imagine that you are a local newspaper reporter. Think about how you would start your report. Write the first four sentences.

3. Compare the two beginnings you have written. What are the main ways in which they differ?

Knowledge

You also need to think about how much your readers know about the subject you are writing about. If they know nothing at all about it, then you will need to give them quite a bit of background information. On the other hand they may know quite a lot. In this case they will become bored if they have to read a lot of stuff they already know.

4. Imagine that you are telling this story to a foreign visitor who knows nothing about foxhunting or about the protests that often happen at hunt meetings. Think about how you would explain this to them. Write the first four sentences of your explanation.

5. Now suppose you were the rider of the horse that fell. Later you tell one of your friends, who was also riding, what happened. How would you tell the story? Write the first four sentences of your account.

Thinking about your audience

Relationship

As you know, we speak to different people differently – according to our relationship with them: you would tell the same story differently if you were speaking to your headteacher and if you were chatting to a close friend. If you are talking to a friend you can use **informal** language. If you do not know the person you are addressing, your language will be more **formal**. Formal and informal language differ in vocabulary and grammar. For example:

formal	**informal**
they will	they'll
Perhaps it is ...	Maybe it's ...
just not true	a load of rubbish

6. Suppose you were the leader of the fire crew trying to rescue the horse. You have to make a report of the incident to your chief back at the station. Write the first four sentences of your report.

7. The same fireman meets one of his mates that evening and tells him about what happened. Write the first four sentences of the story.

Thinking about your audience

Putting it together

You have now thought about the three main questions you need to remember when writing for different audiences. The activities below give you a chance to practise what you have learned. Each one asks you to tell the story of what happened to the horse and its rider, but for a different audience.

Choose two that give you the chance to write very different versions of the same story. For each one, aim to write between 100 and 150 words. Before you start writing, look at the guidelines on page 13.

1. You write the story to be read to a child aged 4 or 5.

2. A journalist writes a report for a local newspaper.

3. A local person saw what happened. He or she writes a regular letter to a friend in the Far East who knows little about British customs. The letter describes what happened and explains the background to it.

4. The leader of the firemen writes a report, to be read by his boss.

5. The Master of Hounds, the leader of the group of foxhunters, writes a report for their monthly newsletter.

6. The hunt protester who telephoned for the emergency services reports on the incident to the next meeting of the animal rights group she belongs to.

7. The rider who was involved in the accident has an elderly relative who worries a lot about her safety when she goes hunting. The rider writes a letter telling her relative about the accident.

Thinking about your audience

Guidelines

Planning and paragraphing

◆ Before you begin writing you need to think about how your audience affects the order in which you write things:

- Do you need to write a lengthy introduction explaining background information?
- Can you do without an introduction and explain things as you go along?

◆ Your audience affects the kind of paragraphs you write:

- Inexperienced readers need information presented in short, simple paragraphs.
- More experienced readers can manage longer and more complicated paragraphs.
- In a report you should keep your paragraphs fairly short.
- In a personal letter you don't have to be so fussy about how long or complicated paragraphs are.

Sentence grammar and vocabulary

◆ Inexperienced readers find it easier to read sentences that are simple and short. When writing for them you should also avoid using long words unless they are essential for your story.

◆ Formal language is suitable for people you do not know, your boss, and other people you want to impress or, at least, not to offend. In formal language you should avoid:

- short forms (write *she will* rather than *she'll*)
- sentences without verbs
- lists like this one
- slangy words and expressions.

◆ Informal language is suitable for friends, relations, and people you get on with well. With them, you can avoid using language that is too formal.

Thinking about purpose

When you write anything you do so for a particular **purpose** – even if it is only to please your English teacher!

These are some of the main purposes for which we write:

We'd only got as far as the top of the cliffs and then it started to rain. We were soaked and we never had a picnic. Had to make do with a burger at the beach café. Some day off!

to persuade

to inform

Why am I writing?

to find out

adjoin

  adjoins the balcony'.
  [AD- + Latin *jungere* to join]
adjourn (*say* a-**jern**) *verb*
  to break off or postpone: 'the meeting was *adjourned* until the next day'.
  Word Family: **adjournment**, *noun*, a) the act of adjourning, b) the state or time of being adjourned.
  [AD- + Latin *diurnus* daily]
adjudicate (*say* a-**joodi**-kate) *verb*
  to judge or settle a dispute, etc.
  Word Family: **adjudication**, *noun*; **adjudicator**, *noun*, a person who adjudicates.
adjunct (*say* **ajjunkt**) *noun*
  something added or attached.
  [Latin *adjunctum* something connected]
adjure (*say* a-**joor**) *verb*
  to solemnly command or request.
  Word Family: **adjuration**, *noun*.
  [AD- + Latin *jurare* to swear]
adjust (*say* a-**just**) *verb*
  1. to change the shape, form or position of something, so that it fits.
  2. to change oneself to match the circumstances: 'it is hard to *adjust* to a new way of life'.
  Word Family: **adjustment**, *noun*; **adjustable**, *adjective*.

to keep a record

to instruct

to get on with people

We enjoyed our stay with you at Epping ever so much. You've got a lovely house and two great kids – I shall never forget Davie's attempts to clean the car! Perhaps later in the year you'll be able to visit us. Miriam's dying to meet you – she's heard so much about you – all of it good of course!!!

to entertain

Can you think of a different example of your own for each of these purposes?

Thinking about purpose

The main part of this unit is based on a true story. It is told in the pictures on this page and the next. Look carefully at the picture story and make sure that you understand clearly what happened. Then turn to page 18.

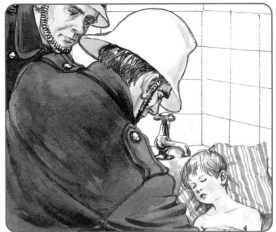

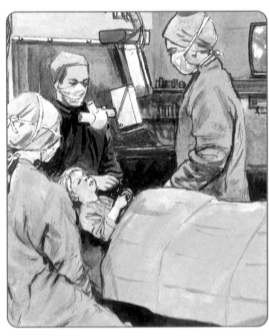

Thinking about purpose

How does it work?

When you write you may have more than one purpose. For example, if you write a letter to a friend you may want to:

◆ keep in touch

◆ give them information

◆ entertain them.

Even so, you will normally have one main purpose. In the next section, we'll look at each of the main purposes in turn.

Finding out

When the boy's mother realized that she couldn't free his finger, she rang the emergency services. The operator asked her a number of questions to find out exactly what had happened. Write the first five lines of the conversation they had. Write it as a script.

Giving information

As the fire engine was on its way, the chief told the others where they were going and what had happened. Write down the first four sentences of what he told them.

Persuading

While the family were waiting for the fire engine, the little boy was getting more and more upset. His mother tried to persuade him to calm down. Write the first five lines of the conversation she had with them. Write it as a script.

Keeping a record

The fire officer who was called to the house had to write down what he saw. Write down the first four sentences of his report.

Instructing

The fire officer realized that they were not going to be able to free the child's finger themselves. So he told the firemen what they had to do. Write down his first four sentences.

Thinking about purpose

Getting on with people

The boy's mother writes a regular weekly letter to her mother, who now lives in Australia. The boy's mother tells her mother all the family news. Write the first four sentences of the letter the boy's mother wrote after this incident.

Entertaining

One of the firemen meets up with his friends most evenings at the pub. That evening he tells them about the incident – as an unusual story to entertain them. Write the first four sentences of what he says.

Putting it together

You have now thought about the main purposes for which we can write. The activities below give you a chance to practise what you have learned. Each one is based on the story of what happened to the little boy in the bath, but each has a different purpose.

Choose two: one from Section A and one from Section B. Before you start writing, look at the guidelines on page 20.

Section A

1. The family claim on their insurance policy for a new bath. The insurance company has to know exactly what happened before it will pay out on their claim. Write a list of all the questions you think the company might ask.

2. Accidents in the home often involve young children. Write a set of simple 'Dos and Don'ts' to help avoid such accidents.

3. A firm puts an advertisement for a 'child-proof' bath in a newspaper or magazine. Write the advertisment.

Section B

4. A journalist writes a report of the incident in the local newspaper. (It has two purposes: to inform the readers and to entertain them.)

5. The fire officer who was called to the scene of the incident writes a report, to be read by his boss.

6. The boy's mother writes to her mother in Australia. Write the complete letter.

Thinking about purpose

Guidelines

Audience

Remember that you not only have to think of **why** you are writing, you also have to remember **who** you are writing for. Each of the writing tasks on page 19 is for a particular audience. Numbers 1, 2, 4 and 5 are quite **formal**, but you can be much more **informal** in numbers 3 and 6.

Planning and paragraphing

Not all writing tasks have to be written in paragraphs. For example, none of the tasks in Section A on page 19 needs to be. But when you are writing in paragraphs, you need to remember your purpose when you plan your writing:

◆ You should make it clear near the beginning what your main purpose is. Sometimes you can just let the reader find this out (as in a personal letter), but often – especially in formal writing – you need a paragraph near the beginning that explains 'what it's all about'.

◆ If you have a very simple purpose, then you need to use short, simple paragraphs. Number 5 on page 19 is an example of this.

◆ Remember that newspaper reports normally use very short paragraphs – these often only have one or two sentences and don't follow the paragraphing guidelines on page 25.

Sentence grammar and vocabulary

◆ It is particularly important to match your vocabulary to your purpose. If you're selling a car you describe it in a different way from the policeman who is describing a car that has been stolen!

◆ This is also true of the way you build your sentences. Rules and advertisements both call for short, simple sentences. A personal letter, on the other hand, can use much longer sentences. Think carefully about your purpose and your audience when building sentences.

Writing in paragraphs

If you write more than a few sentences about a subject, you will probably need to arrange your sentences into **paragraphs**.

Why we use paragraphs

We organize writing into paragraphs for these reasons:

◆ It helps us as we write, because it makes us group together sentences about the same topic.

◆ It makes us think about the best order for our sentences.

◆ It breaks our writing into sections which make life easier for the reader.

Parts of a paragraph

The lead sentence
This is the first or second sentence of the paragraph. It tells us what the paragraph is going to be about.

> It was the stormiest night I can remember.

The body of the paragraph
This is a group of sentences that follow the lead sentence – and tell the reader more about the subject.

> The wind howled all night and as I lay in bed I could hear branches crashing from the trees. Rain lashed against the windows almost without a break. Brilliant flashes of lightning were followed by terrifying peals of thunder. I tossed and turned in bed thinking of poor Midge, lost somewhere in the forest.

The concluding sentence
This is the last sentence in the paragraph. It sums up what you have said in the paragraph and rounds it off.

> I hardly slept a wink.

Writing in paragraphs

Linking paragraphs together

If possible, you should make your writing 'flow' from one paragraph to the next. The following paragraph, for example, could continue in a number of ways:

> It was the stormiest night I can remember. The wind howled all night and as I lay in bed I could hear branches crashing from the trees. Rain lashed against the windows almost without a break. Brilliant flashes of lightning were followed by terrifying peals of thunder. I tossed and turned in bed thinking of poor Midge, lost somewhere in the forest. I hardly slept a wink.

> The next day I got up early to survey the damage.

1

> I need not have worried.

2

> I had let Midge out that evening for a run in the yard.

3

Each of the sentences in the numbered boxes is the lead sentence for the next paragraph. Each of them refers back to things in the previous paragraph:

1. This sentence uses 'I' – so we know it's the same person telling the story. It talks about 'the next day' – because the first paragraph was about the night. And it refers to 'the damage', which was also described in the first paragraph.

2. This sentence also uses 'I'. It talks about being 'worried' – which the storyteller described in more detail in the first paragraph.

3. This is also about 'I'. It refers back to the storyteller's worries about Midge, described towards the end of the first paragraph.

There are many different ways in which you can link paragraphs together. Often this just happens naturally as you write. But when you read through what you have written in a first draft, you should make sure that the links are there. If they aren't, rewrite your paragraphs to include them.

Writing in paragraphs

Exercise A

1. Choose one of the lead sentences in the numbered boxes on page 22. Write the whole paragraph from which it might come. Make sure that your paragraph follows the guidelines on page 21.

2. Now do the same for one of the other two lead sentences.

3. Now use some of the ideas you have developed to write a series of four paragraphs following on from the paragraph quoted on page 21. Follow the guidelines given on pages 21 and 22.

Other ways of linking paragraphs

There is a group of words and phrases you can use to show that one paragraph follows on from the next. These are called **adverbials** and there is more about them on pages 123–4.

Time

You can use adverbials to show **when** things happen in this paragraph as compared with the last:

> the next day
> at about the same time
> meanwhile

Cause and effect

You can also show that what you are writing about in this paragraph was **caused by** what happened in the last one:

> as a result
> therefore
> because of this

Place

You can do a similar thing when writing about **where** things happen in this paragraph as compared with the last:

> nearby
> in the distance
> elsewhere in the same village

Contrast

You can do the opposite, by using adverbials that show this paragraph and the last one are definitely not **linked** in this way:

> even so
> on the other hand
> by contrast

Writing in paragraphs

Exercise B

Read the text that follows. Work out *all* the ways in which the paragraphs are linked together. Write them down.

Water has put its mark on several stages in my life. One of them was long before the Navy, when my family moved from the North to the flat Fens of East Anglia. It was two years before the war, and I was twelve.

My father, who was a teacher and part-time tobacconist in his own father's shop, brought us south when his school had to cut back its staff and he had lost his job. He went ahead of us to his new school in Wisbech, and my mother brought the rest of us to join him some months later.

I remember my mother's anxiety. She had wept when she was scrubbing the bare floorboards of our empty house in Jarrow to leave it clean for the new people, and all through the journey she fretted over her four children. I was the eldest, with two young brothers and a little sister, a small herd of Geordies who knew nothing about where we were going.

My grandfather had told me, 'They grow so much fruit down there, man, that you'll be able to pluck bananas from the hedges.' What he had never said was that the Fens were flat.

Every scrap of variety drained out of the landscape as we came to the Fens just as the sun was going down. The land was so flat we could have been on an inland lake, and the view out of every window was so utterly changeless that our train seemed to stop moving long before it drew into Wisbech. It was the platform itself that seemed to come out of the dark and haul itself alongside us like an old barge, clanking and hissing.

Writing in paragraphs

Guidelines

◆ We use paragraphs:

- to help us organize our writing
- to make our writing easier for the reader to follow.

◆ Each paragraph should begin with a **lead sentence** – normally the first or second sentence.

◆ The sentences that follow the lead sentence should tell us more about the subject of the paragraph. These are called the **body of the paragraph**.

◆ The paragraph should end with a **concluding sentence**. This sums up what the paragraph says and rounds it off.

◆ Each paragraph should be **linked** to the one that goes before by:

- subject matter, or
- the use of words that have been used in the paragraph before, or
- pronouns, or
- adverbials – of time, place, reason or contrast.

Telling a story

We see, hear or read stories every day of our lives.

You'll never guess what happened today –

Talking points

1. What kind of stories do we listen to rather than read?

2. What kind of stories do we see rather than read?

3. How many different kinds of written story can you think of?

4. Most people like stories. Why do you think this is?

Caught in the storm

On the next page there is a sequence of pictures. They tell the beginning and the end of a story, but the middle is missing. It is shown by a question mark. Look at the pictures carefully and work out what they show. What might happen in the missing part of the story? If possible, think of more than one answer to this question.

Telling a story

Viewpoint

You can tell a story in many different ways. You have a number of choices and one of the most important is the viewpoint. Compare these three short extracts:

A

Well, here I am again, sitting outside the Principal's office. And I've only been at the school for two days. Two lots of trouble in two days! Yesterday I got the strap for nothing. Nothing at all.

B

'Is that where we live?' said Lehman.

They both looked at the tumbledown hut on top of the hill. 'We'll fix it up in no time', said Dad. 'It'll soon be like it was in the old days. When I first came here. As good as new.'

And after a while it was. It was home. Lehman became used to it.

C

The question is: did the girl kill her own father? Some say yes and some say no.

Linda doesn't look like a murderess.

She walks calmly up the steps of the high school stage. She shakes the mayor's hand and receives her award. Top of the school.

Exercise A

1. Whose voice do we hear in Extract A? What sort of person do you think they are?
2. Whose voice do we hear in Extract B? From whose point of view are we seeing the story?
3. Whose voice do we hear in Extract C? From whose point of view are we seeing the story?

Three different viewpoints

These three extracts illustrate three different ways of telling a story:

1. You can tell it as if you were the main character, writing as 'I'.
2. You can follow the main character through the story and describe what they do, think and feel. You write of the character as 'he' or 'she'.
3. You can be further away from the things you are describing – as if you were a giant looking down on the story. You don't just follow one story, you treat the main characters equally.

Telling a story

Exercise B

1. Look at the first two pictures of the picture story on page 27. Decide exactly what is happening in them.

2. Write the beginning of the story as if you were the girl in the pictures. Write as 'I'. Include:

   • what she did
   • what she thought
   • how she felt.

   Just write one paragraph.

3. Now write a second version. Change the first one, so that instead of writing 'I', 'me', 'mine' and so on, you write 'she', 'her' and 'hers'.

4. Now look again at the two pictures. They show the girl and her mother. Think about how you would tell the story if you wanted to give the same attention to the girl and her mother. Write two short paragraphs, one telling us about the girl, and the other about her mother.

5. Read through what you have written. Think about:

   • the different information there is in each version
   • the different atmosphere each one has
   • which one you like best and why.

Where shall I start?

It might seem obvious: begin at the beginning, go on until you get to the end and then stop. In fact you don't have to begin at the beginning when you tell a story. For example, you could start the story we are working on in any of these places:

   • at the beginning
   • at the point where the tree falls on the car
   • at the moment when the mother is rescued.

If you were telling it from the point of view of one of the emergency workers, you could start at the point where the emergency call comes in.

1. Think of the place you would like to start telling this story. You can choose any point you like, *but not the beginning!* You can choose whatever viewpoint you like.

2. Write the first paragraph of the story.

Telling a story

The ingredients of a story

Good stories don't just tell you what happened. They are about other things, too:

Dad was scabbing around in the rubbish. ←———— **1 Actions**

'How embarrassing,' said Pete, 'It's
lucky there's no one else here to see us.' ←———— **2 Speech**

I looked around the tip. He was right.
No one was dumping rubbish except us.
There was just Dad, me and my twin
brother Pete. The man driving the
bulldozer didn't count. He was probably ←———— **3 Thoughts**
used to people coming to the tip with
junk and then taking a whole pile of
stuff back home.

It was a huge tip with a large, muddy ←———— **4 Description**
pond in the middle …

Exercise D

You have now written a number of beginnings for your story.

1. Read them through again and decide which one you like the best.

2. You are now going to write a continuation of the one you have chosen.

3. Make a plan showing the order in which you will tell the story. Do it like this:

> *1 They leave the house.*
> *2 The wind is very strong. They drive along the road …*

4. If you aren't starting at the beginning you will have to work out when to tell readers 'the story so far' – what happened *before* the starting point. You can do this in one lump, or in a series of shorter pieces. Mark this on your plan.

5. Look through your plan and check where you have places for:
- speech
- thoughts
- description.

Mark these on your plan.

6. Now write your story.

Telling a story

Guidelines

Audience and purpose

Your first purpose in writing a story is to entertain your readers. If you don't entertain them, they will feel disappointed and stop reading. A good way of thinking about your readers is to think of yourself. Ask yourself, 'What kind of story do *I* like reading?' Imagine that you are writing for readers just like you.

Paragraphing

There is detailed information about paragraphing on page 25. Remember these points when writing a story:

◆ Start a new paragraph when a new person speaks.

◆ Don't make your paragraphs too long. It is a good idea to start a new paragraph when:

- a character appears for the first time
- an important new stage of the story arrives
- there has been a gap of time that you are not describing.

Sentence grammar

One of the most important things when writing a story is to make sure that you get your **verbs** right:

◆ Most stories are told using **past** tenses. The **present** tense is used in direct speech. Only tell your story in the present tense if you want to make a very special effect.

◆ When you finish writing, check your verbs to make sure that you have used the **correct form of the past tense**.

(There is more about this on page 112.)

When you are in the middle of writing the story it is very easy to write several sentences using a string of ... *and* ... *and* ... *and* ..., or ... *then* ... *then* ... *then* ... (or even ... *and then* ... *and then* ...). Vary your sentences by using **conjunctions** like *when, after, before, while, as, until*.

(There is more about this on pages 107 and 127–30.)

A5 Writing a description

Sometimes you may be asked to write a description on its own. Often you find you need to include description as part of a longer piece of writing – a story, for example. In this unit you will look at ways of describing places, people and things.

Think about:

◆ what you find interesting about this scene

◆ how you might describe it

◆ what you might find difficult to describe.

Writing a description

Using your senses

When you write a description, you should try to use as many of your senses as you can. Often people only use one or two.

Hearing – think about:

- volume (loud/soft)
- pitch (high/low)
- rhythm.

Words like:

whispering, ear-splitting, booming, gentle, sizzle, click, buzzing, echoing, deep, booming, clashing

Sight – think about:

- shape
- colour
- size
- pattern.

Words like:

round, square, lumpy, purple, emerald, high, tiny, enormous, slender, striped

Smell – think about:

- strength
- type
- pleasantness.

Words like:

fragrant, stinking, sweet, clinging, spicy, fumes, gas, petrol, smoky, musty, rotten, violets, ozone, decay

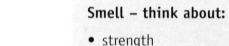
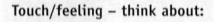

Touch/feeling – think about:

- texture (rough/smooth)
- temperature
- dry/wet.

Words like:

silky, velvety, harsh, dusty, gritty, icy, warm, burning, sticky, chilled, damp, soaking, parched

Taste – think about:

- sweet/sour/savoury
- strong/weak
- mild/spicy.

Words like:

sharp, tart, bitter, salty, stale, pungent, peppery, minty, treacly, vinegary, rotten, delicious, tasteless

Writing a description

Exercise A

You are going to write a description of the place in the picture on page 32. Imagine that you have visited it while on holiday and want to describe it in a letter to a friend.

You will work in three stages:

◆ thinking

◆ organizing

◆ writing.

Thinking

A: Using your senses

1. Look carefully at the city shown in the picture and imagine that you are actually there.

2. Write down a list of all the things you can see:
   - Don't write whole sentences, just words and phrases.
   - Don't stick to just what is in the picture; imagine what else you might see if you were there.

3. Now make similar lists for what you can:
   - hear
   - smell
   - feel
   - taste.

B: Making comparisons

It often helps a description if you can compare the thing you are describing to something else. A sentence like this immediately makes a vivid picture in your mind:

> She had hair like mouldy hay.

4. Go through the lists you have written. Pick out five of the words or phrases you have listed. For each one make a comparison to help the reader get a clear picture of what you are describing.

Writing a description

Organizing

Sometimes it is difficult to know how to organize your description:

◆ Where do you start?

◆ In what order do you describe things?

◆ How do you finish?

Here are some suggestions:

5. You can imagine you are walking through the picture and describe what you see as you go.

6. You can decide what your strongest feeling is about the scene (for example, excitement at the brightly coloured and dazzling lights). Use that as the beginning of your description and come back to it again at the end.

7. You can think of one word to sum up your impressions of this place. Use that word in each of your paragraphs as you describe an aspect of the scene.

8. Look at your lists again and think about the order in which you will use the ideas in them. Cross out any ideas you are not going to use. Put numbers beside the things that are left to show the order in which you will use them. It will probably help to make a short plan with just one or two words showing what will be in each paragraph.

Writing

9. Now write your description.

Writing a description

Exercise B

Now it's time to describe a person. Choose one of the people on this page:

Thinking

1. Look carefully at the picture you have chosen. Try to get a clear picture of this person in your mind. Imagine how they move, speak and behave with other people.

2. Go through the list of questions in the box on the next page. Make notes on your answers. Answer as many of the questions as you can, but don't waste too much time on ones you cannot answer.

3. Add notes on any other things about the person that you think are important.

Writing a description

Organizing

4. Now you are going to think about how to organize your description of this person. Imagine that you have met this person and he or she made a big impression on you. You are writing a letter to a friend and want to include a description. Make a short plan of the main things you want to say and the order in which you want to say them.

Writing

5. Now write your description.

Questions

Head

1. What shape is the *face*: fat, thin, round, square, oval … ?

2. Is the *skin* smooth, lined, creased, weathered … ?

3. What about the *hair*: long, short, straight, curly, blonde, grey … ?

4. What colour and shape are the *eyes*: blue, grey, brown, thin, wide, beady, milky … ?

5. Is the *nose* large, long, snub, fat, hooked, prominent, pointed … ?

6. How would you describe the *mouth and lips*: fleshy, full, thin, mean, smiling, pouting … ?

Hands and fingers

7. Would you describe them as: thin, smooth, wrinkled, fine, fat, muscular, elegant, strong, feeble, stumpy, pointed … ?

Body

8. Is the body chunky, fat, lean, squat, podgy, scrawny, slender, stocky, scrawny, thickset … ?

Posture and movement

9. When the person is sitting or standing, is their *position:* straight, slumped, sagging, stiff, relaxed, strong, weak … ?

10. How do they *move:* confidently, swiftly, slowly, jerkily, clumsily, elegantly … ?

Comparisons

11. If this person were an animal, what animal would they be?

12. If the person were a car, what car would they be?

13. When you look at them, is there anything else they remind you of?

Writing a description

Guidelines

Purpose

Often a description forms part of a larger piece of writing; for example, a story or an explanation. If so, you need to be clear *why* it is needed.

◆ In a **story** the reader may need to know what one of the characters looks like, or to understand what it is like to be in a particular place. If you make your description too long readers will get bored – so keep it **brief**.

◆ In an **explanation** the purpose of description is to give readers information, so that they can understand the rest of the writing. So descriptions need to be **clear**.

◆ You may be asked to write **a description that stands on its own**. In this case your purpose is to write **interestingly and entertainingly**.

Paragraphing

Probably the hardest thing in writing a good description is how to organize it. It's not like a story, where things happen in order. If you're describing something it is all there at the same time! In what order should you describe different features? Three good ways are:

◆ **Walk through it**

If you are describing a place, imagine yourself walking through or around it. If it is a person, begin with the face and work downwards.

◆ **'A day in the life'**

Sometimes you can spread your description over a period of time. This works well when you are describing a place: *At six in the morning the High Street is quiet. Nothing stirs except for the odd stray cat ...*

◆ **Think of a theme**

A place may give you a particular feeling. If so, it is a good idea to use this as the theme of your description: *Everything about Brentwood is dull, uniform, and modern. The shops all look the same, the houses ...* You can do the same with a description of a person: *Mr Martell reminded her of an elderly eagle. He had a large hooked nose, just like a beak ...*

Sentence grammar

Verb tenses are important in a description. In a story a description will usually be written using **past** tenses (*Mr Martell **reminded** her of an elderly eagle. He **had** ...*). A description that stands on its own will often need the **present** tense (*Everything about Brentwood **is** dull, uniform, and modern. The shops all **look** ...*).

Explanations and instructions

A

In an emergency call

999

1 Lift the telephone handset and **PRESS OR DIAL 999**. **112** may also be used as an alternative to **999**

2 Tell the BT operator – **WHICH EMERGENCY SERVICE YOU WANT**

3 Wait for the BT operator to connect you to the Emergency Service

4 Tell the Emergency Service – **WHERE THE TROUBLE IS WHAT THE TROUBLE IS WHERE YOU ARE** and the number of the phone you are using.

B

Saving lives

It will not be long before a paramedic will be able to receive on-the-spot expert advice at the scene of an accident. The paramedic will be able to look at a diagram showing him or her exactly what to do. The life-saving equipment is a combination of video-conferencing software and a satellite communications network.

C

PICTIONARY is the rousing and classic board game that is played like charades, only on paper. Instead of acting, you and your team-mates try to guess various words and phrases by sketching clues to each other.

PREPARATION

Place the timer and card boxes so that all players have access to them. Divide equally into teams of two to four.

Instructions

Instructions tell the reader what to do. They are written in the correct order and are often numbered, like Example A.

Explanations

Explanations tell the reader what something is like or how it works. An explanation is different from a description. A description tells you what something looks, sounds, tastes, smells or feels like. An explanation like Example B helps you *understand* what it is like.

A mixture

Often instructions and explanations go together. Example C, which is taken from the rules of a game, shows you how this works.

Explanations and instructions

Instructions

Exercise A

Use these notes to write a set of instructions explaining how to make a pot of tea. Make sure that you write in complete sentences:

> water ⟶ kettle
> switch on
> get teapot
> kettle boils
> switch off
> a little water ⟶ teapot
> warm teapot
> empty
> put in teabags (1/person)
> water in
> wait 2 minutes
> stir
> wait 1 minute
> get cups
> add milk (if wanted)
> pour tea

When you have finished writing, read the instructions through and make sure that everything is clear.

Exercise B

Of course most people know how to make tea, but we often have to give instructions to someone who really doesn't know the information we are giving.

1. Think of a public building (for example, a shop, post office, police station, bus station).

2. Write clear instructions on how to get to it from your school.

3. When you have finished writing them, check through to make sure they are clear.

Could you tell me the way to the nearest post office, please?

Explanations and instructions

An explanation

Your school is going to be visited by some students from Thailand. They all speak English well, but the schools in their country are very different from yours. You have been asked to write a short explanation of what English schools are like.

Exercise C

1. Asking questions

The first thing to do is to think about what the students would like to know. Try making a list of the questions they might want answers to. For example:

- At what age do children start at your school?
- How many pupils are there at the school?
- How many classes are there in each year?

Make a list of at least five questions to answer.

2. Making notes

Now make a set of short answers to your questions. Don't write whole sentences; write as briefly as you can. As you make your notes, add in any extra information you think of.

3. Making a plan

Now list three or four main headings for your explanation. You can think of your own, or choose from these:

- ages and classes
- subjects
- exams and tests
- discipline
- facts and figures
- teachers
- daily timetable
- terms and holidays.

4. Preparing to write

You're going to write one paragraph for each heading. Look at the notes you made and work out which information will go into each paragraph.

5. Writing a draft

Use your headings and notes to write three or four paragraphs.

6. Checking and redrafting

Read through what you have written. Check it against the guidelines on page 43. In particular think about the **audience** you are writing for. Make any changes needed.

Explanations and instructions

Same subject, different audiences

How you explain something depends very much on the person you are explaining it to. For the next exercises you need to choose a subject that you know quite a lot about, but which other people may not understand at all. Try to choose something that is an interest of yours. The picture suggests two possibilities, but you can choose your own topic.

Exercise D

An elderly person has asked you to explain your interest to her. She doesn't want to be able to *do* whatever is involved, but she'd like to know what it is and roughly how it works (or what you do). Write a short explanation for her.

Before you write, think about:

◆ the things she will find most difficult to understand – these will take more time to explain
◆ any special words you need to use which she may not understand – work out how to explain them
◆ the order to explain things in.

Exercise E

Now you are going to write about the same subject, but for a different audience. A friend doesn't share your interest, but would like to know more. He or she would like you to explain about it and then give some basic instructions about what to do. (So, for example, if it is a computer game, you need to explain what the game is, what the aim of it is, and how you play it.)

Before you write, think about:

◆ how you would sum up what is really interesting about the topic
◆ the main features you need to explain
◆ questions your friend is likely to ask.

You could also think about whether it would help to add drawings or diagrams and captions to your explanation.

Explanations and instructions

Guidelines

Audience and purpose

When you are writing an explanation or instructions it is very important to think carefully about your audience. In particular you should ask yourself:

◆ How much (or how little) do they know about this subject?

◆ So where should I begin my explanation?

◆ Are there special words which I need to explain?

◆ How slowly and carefully should I go to make sure I don't lose them?

In both explanations and instructions, it is very important to make sure that you get things in the right **order**. If you don't your readers will quickly lose track.

Paragraphing

There is detailed information about paragraphing on page 25. Remember these points when writing an explanation:

◆ Break your subject down into small sections. Give each section one or two paragraphs.

◆ Make it clear in the lead sentence exactly what the paragraph is about.

◆ Try to include explanations of special words as you go along. For example, *The throatlash is the part of the bridle that goes from the headpiece round the pony's throat.*

◆ Begin with an introductory paragraph that tells the reader a little bit about how you are going to cover the subject. For example, *We will begin by looking at the things that make a mountain bike special and then go on to some of the places where you can ride them. After that ...*

Sentence grammar

◆ The **verbs** in an explanation are usually in the **present tense**. (See pages 111–12.)

◆ When you write instructions you often need use **directives** (also called 'commands'). You need to take care with this kind of sentence. If you make them too much like commands and there are too many of them, you begin to sound rather bossy.

Argument and persuasion

Words can be the most powerful things when you want to persuade someone to agree with you, or to do something for you. Look at this invented advertisement.

A touch of old-fashioned luxury ...

Do you ever long for the days when motoring <u>was</u> motoring? – The open road, the rush of wind in your hair, the surge of raw power at your command ...

CRANK 1

If you do, then this is <u>your</u> car

the Crank Wagon 2000 sri

Exercise A

1. What kind of person is this advertisement aimed at?

2. What makes you think this?

3. How does it try to attract people to the car? Quote words or phrases to explain what you mean.

4. Adverts like this paint a picture of the product and of the kind of person you could become if you bought it. They don't contain many facts, but rely on the **power of words** to have their effect. Make a list of TV or printed adverts that work in this way.

Argument and persuasion

Other advertisements try to persuade you by giving you information. Look at this invented advertisement and then answer the questions at the bottom of the page.

the BangerMobile 'City'

- the shopping bag on wheels
- cheaper to run than a pushbike
- parking? no problem – it turns on a pinhead
- room in the back for your growing family

The car for the working mum

Exercise B

1. What kind of person is this advertisement aimed at?

2. What makes you think this?

3. How does it try to attract people to the car? Quote words or phrases to explain what you mean.

4. Adverts like this use the **power of facts** to persuade you to buy the product. They often give you a list of the main selling points of the product. Make a list of TV or printed adverts that work in this way.

Exercise C

Choose a product. It can be real or made up. Think up two advertisements for it. The first should rely on the power of words; the second should rely on the power of facts.

Argument and persuasion

Putting a point of view

Expressing an opinion is quite like advertising. On this page and the next we look at the process stage by stage.

Exercise D

A: Know your product

A lot of writers fail because they haven't really worked out what they think before they start to write.

1. Choose a topic that you have an opinion about. Either think of your own, or choose from this list:

   - 'Favourites': football teams, singers, TV programmes ...
   - 'Pet hates': think of your own!
   - 'They should do something about it': cruelty to animals, traffic congestion, pollution ...
   - 'I really believe in': children's rights, vegetarianism, the right to roam ...

2. Make *very brief* notes summing up what you think.

B: The power of words

3. Make a list of words to use when writing about your chosen topic. Choose words that:

   - communicate your opinion (*parking? no problem*)
   - are strong (*... the surge of raw power ...*)
   - will work on people's imaginations (*... the rush of wind in your hair ...*)
   - will communicate or arouse emotion (*... a touch of old-fashioned luxury ...*).

4. Now write four or five short sentences about your topic, using the words you have chosen. Your aim is not to give reasons or have an argument. What you want to do is persuade people to agree with you because of the power of your words.

C: The power of facts

5. Make a list of facts to back up your opinion about the topic. (If you want to see how this is done, look back at the car advert on page 45.)

6. Now write four or five sentences about your topic using the facts you have listed. Your aim now is to persuade readers by the strength of your argument. Make sure that each of the reasons you give is clear and factual.

Argument and persuasion

Building an argument

So far, you've tried out two different ways of putting a point of view. Now you're going to build these into a complete argument.

Opinions and arguments

In written English, the word 'argument' is used to describe a piece of writing that expresses an opinion and then sets out the reasons behind it. If you write a good argument, the reader:

◆ understands clearly why you hold that point of view
◆ is persuaded to agree with you (you hope!).

Exercise E

For this exercise, you can either write about the topic you chose for Exercise D, or think of a new one.

Planning

1. Write a clear statement of the opinion you are going to express.

2. Make a list of all the reasons why you hold that opinion and think it is right.

3. You're going to write two paragraphs that explain the reasons behind your opinion. Look at the list of reasons and work out how to arrange them into two groups. Write the reasons in two lists; put them in order so that one leads on to the next.

Writing the main argument

4. Write two paragraphs based on the lists you have made.

Writing the introduction and conclusion

5. Now you have to think of a way of introducing your argument. Write a short paragraph to do this.

6. Write a final short paragraph that rounds the argument off – and finally persuades your readers that they just have to agree with you!

> 1   Traffic should be banned from the town centre

> 2
> 1. traffic jams morning and evening
> 2. fumes and pollution
> 3. dangerous for pedestrians

> 3
> A
> - roads narrow
> - traffic jams
> - morning + evening
> - ambulances can't get to hospital
>
> B
> - no space for pedestrians
> - fumes and pollution

> 4   The roads through the centre of town are narrow. This means that during the morning and evening rush hours there are long traffic jams. Ambulances and

> 5   Every summer tourists come to Wyedean in their thousands. Yet for many the visit is spoiled by the traffic in the town centre. They cannot see

> 6   We need to make the town centre a pedestrian zone. All traffic should be sent round the inner ring road. Then

Argument and persuasion

Guidelines

Audience and purpose

In this unit we have concentrated on purpose: *why* you are writing – to persuade. It is also very important to think of your audience. Think about:

◆ **How much they know about the subject**

This will help you to work out how much you need to tell them about the background. For example, if you are writing about traffic jams in your local town, you don't have to describe them to local people – they already know what they are like! Outsiders, on the other hand, need a description of how bad the traffic jams can be.

◆ **The best way of persuading them to agree with you**

You need to use different tactics for different audiences. If you are writing an argument about homework to be read by other students, you can take a different approach from one that would work for teachers!

◆ **The right 'tone of voice' to use**

Some audiences like you to be relaxed and casual in your writing. Others would be put off if they thought you were being too casual.

Paragraphing

Remember that there is detailed information about paragraphing on page 25.

The most important thing to remember when planning an argument is that one reason should lead on naturally to the next. You will save yourself a lot of trouble if you make a written plan before you start writing.

Sentence grammar

◆ Take care with your **verbs**. You will need a mixture of **tenses**. If you're describing things that have already happened, you'll need past tenses. You may also need future tenses if you're predicting what *will* happen. You will certainly need to talk about things that are true *now* – so you'll need present tenses as well.

There is more about tenses on pages 111–12.

◆ Arguments often use sentences containing words like *if, unless* and *although*. There is more about sentences containing these words on pages 129–30.

◆ When you are giving reasons for things you'll need conjunctions like *since, because, as* (see page 128) and sentence adverbials like *for this reason, as a result* and *in spite of this*. (See pages 123–4.)

Writing a letter

These days – with emails, telephones and faxes – you might think there's no need to write letters. But people still send and receive millions of letters every day.

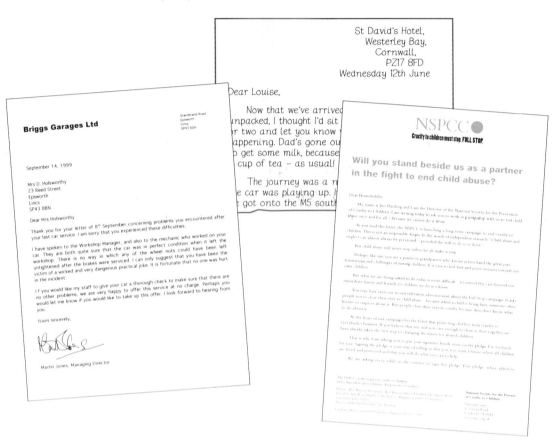

This unit looks at how to write two kinds of letter that you may need to send:

- **personal letters**

  These are letters you write to people you know or have met. They are usually about things to do with your own life. An example is a letter to family or friends when you are away from home, telling them about your experiences.

- **business letters**

  These are written to people you do not know, and they are usually written to achieve a particular goal. Examples are job application letters, letters of complaint about a product, and letters to a newspaper.

Writing a letter

A personal letter

Most personal letters follow a similar pattern. These are the main parts of a personal letter:

Your address

St David's Hotel,
Westerley Bay,
Cornwall,
PZ17 8FD
Wednesday 12th June   ← **Date**

Greeting → Dear Louise,

Now that we've arrived safely and unpacked, I thought I'd sit down for a minute or two and let you know what's been happening. Dad's gone out to find somewhere to get some milk, because we're both dying for a cup of tea – as usual!   ← **Introductory paragraph**

The journey was a nightmare, because the car

body of the letter

looking forward to a break – it's the first proper holiday Dad and I have had for over five years. I feel a bit bad about leaving you and Melanie to cope on your own, but as Dad keeps telling me you're both big girls now!

Don't forget to water those plants in the living room – and do drop us a line if you've got a moment. Take care, both of you.   ← **Concluding paragraph**

Ending → All our love,

Mum

Parts of a personal letter

Your address

People usually put this in full – especially if they are at an address that the other person doesn't know. You can set it out in one of two ways:

indented
St David's Hotel,
Westerley Bay,
Cornwall,
PZ17 8FD

square
St David's Hotel,
Westerley Bay,
Cornwall,
PZ17 8FD

Each word begins with a capital letter. Put a comma at the end of each line and after the house number if there is one. Put a full stop at the end.

Date

In a personal letter this is usually put as either 'Wednesday 12th June', for example, or simply 'Wednesday'.

Greeting

You usually use the name you use when you are talking to the person: a first name or nickname if you know them well; or a title ('Mr/Mrs' etc.) and surname if you want to be polite to someone you do not know very well.

Introductory paragraph

It is usually a good idea to have a short paragraph to 'get the letter started'. This is like the beginning of a conversation, where you say things like, 'How are you?' and 'What have you been doing recently?'

Body of the letter

This is the main part, where you include all your news. Not everyone bothers to divide it into paragraphs, but it helps the reader if you do.

Concluding paragraph

This is where you say 'goodbye' and round the letter off.

Ending

If you are writing to family or friends you can choose whatever ending you like. If the letter is to someone you do not know well and you want to be polite, you could use 'Yours sincerely,' followed by your first name and surname. 'With best wishes,' followed by the same signature, is slightly less formal, but still polite.

Imagine that you are Louise in the letter on the previous page. While your parents are away, all sorts of things go wrong. Write one of these letters:

◆ to a friend who used to live near you, but has moved away, telling her what has happened
◆ to your parents, making light of what has happened.

Writing a letter

A business letter

Letters like this are usually written to someone working in a company or organization. They are often kept (filed) so that other people can read them again later. So these letters are less personal and more formal. They also have to have extra features.

Your address →

Seagull Travel Ltd
100-105 The Walk
Maudesley
WK3 7DQ

Their address →

Mr P. Barnes
Headteacher
Maryton School
James Street
Lyddon
KN7 9DS

Date →

2nd February 1999

Greeting →

Dear Mr Barnes,

Introductory paragraph →

You wrote to us recently enquiring about sponsorship for projects at your school.

I have now discussed your proposal with our Board of Directors and they have agreed that they are willing

body of the letter

school project. £1000 will go to the project and a prize of £100 to the writer of the letter.

Concluding paragraph →

I hope you and your staff will find this helpful. If you have any further questions, please do not hesitate to contact me.

Ending →

Yours sincerely,

P.F. Marriott

P.F. Marriott, Marketing Director

Writing a letter

Parts of a business letter

Your address

This is usually placed square, as in the example, not indented. In business letters it is quite normal not to put in commas or full stops.

Their address

You put the name of the person you are writing to and their job. This makes sure that the letter gets to the right person, even if it is opened by someone else. Normally you also put their full address.

Date

This should include the day, month and year. '2nd February 1999' is better than 2/2/99.

Greeting

If you know the surname of the person you are writing to, then use it. For a man use 'Mr'. If you are writing to a woman and know that she prefers to be addressed as 'Mrs', 'Miss' or 'Ms', then use that form. Otherwise use 'Ms'. If you don't know the surname of the person you are writing to, then begin, 'Dear Sir or Madam'.

Introductory paragraph

Write one or two sentences explaining what the letter is about. This helps the person you are writing to. They can organize their correspondence by subject and then deal with things in order.

Body of the letter

This should be divided into fairly short paragraphs. There is more about this on page 55.

Concluding paragraph

You should aim to leave the reader in a good frame of mind. If you want them to do something, you can politely remind them of this. If you want a reply, you can use a sentence like, 'I look forward to hearing from you'.

Ending

If you started with 'Dear Ms _____', 'Dear Mr _____', etc., then end 'Yours sincerely,' followed by your initials and surname. If you started with 'Dear Sir or Madam,' then end 'Yours faithfully,' followed by your initials and surname. After your signature, print your name if the signature is at all difficult to read. If you have a job title, then this should be written after the signature as well.

Writing a letter

Exercise B

Win your school £1000

Seagull Travel is offering to sponsor a 'school project' with a gift of £1000. The project could be to improve something that already exists, like the school library or a sports team, or it could be for a new idea, such as a nature reserve on the school grounds. Seagull Travel will decide what to sponsor by judging letters sent in by students at the school. The best letter will win the **£1000** sponsorship for its chosen project, plus a personal prize of **£100** for the letter-writer.

1. Think of a project in your school that you want sponsorship for. It could be a real project or one that you have made up.

2. Make a list of 'selling points' – reasons why you think this project is worth sponsorship.

3. Organize your selling points into three groups. These will be the three paragraphs in the body of the letter.

4. Write a first draft of the letter, starting with the greeting. Follow the pattern on page 52:

   - introduction
   - body (three paragraphs)
   - conclusion.

5. Check your draft and change it as necessary.

6. Write a final version with all the parts of the letter (addresses, date, and so on).

Writing a letter

Guidelines

Audience and purpose

Personal letters are usually written:

◆ to entertain

◆ to keep in touch.

Business letters are often written:

◆ to give information

◆ to persuade people to do something.

It is very important to think clearly about your audience, especially in business letters. Your letter will probably be read by someone you have never met, so it is a mistake to be too casual in the way you write. Remember that the reader may not know much about the particular subject you are writing about and may have to answer dozens of letters every day. Keep it clear; keep it simple.

Paragraphing

In a business letter you should always have a short paragraph of **introduction** and a short paragraph of **conclusion**. The **body of the letter** should have at least one paragraph. Try to keep your paragraphs fairly short – about five or six sentences. If in doubt, divide a longer paragraph into two shorter ones.

Writing a report

In Unit 1 you worked on writing stories of different kinds. This unit is about *factual* stories and how they are reported. There are different kinds of report:

Use of office photocopiers

Report by James Lee

Summary

I was asked by Senior Management to report on the use made of office photocopiers, to see how efficiently we were using our resources and to find out where savings could be made. I was assisted in this work by Angela Rees and Michel Hewett.

In general we found that most members of staff used the available equipment sensibly and without undue waste. There were a few exceptions to this and we have a number of recommendations to avoid future waste.

The equipment

The office has a total of five photoc... ...s of different types, brands and sizes. This variet... because they all use the same pap... has been contracted out to a sing... other hand it means that we hav... different types of toner, which is... we just had to keep a larger sto...

Use of office photocopiers

Scandon 1st XI v. Nesford High School XI, 3rd February 2000

RESULT: Scandon 3 Nesford 0

Scorers: Peter Davies (2) Darren Tyke (1)

The first half was evenly matched and after 20 minutes Nesford came near to scoring. Scandon defence held firm, with good work by Andie Gadd and Mark Litton. Towards the end of the half, we began to get more forward possession. The second half was all Scandon. After 12 minutes Darren Tyke made a run down the right wing and set Peter Davies up for his first scoring chance. Peter's second goal was a solo effort, after a free kick taken by Martin Highfield. In the last minute of the match Darren Tyke headed in from close range.

In this unit you will look at two types of report:

◆ newspaper reports

◆ more formal reports.

Writing a report

Sorting out the facts

Before you can tell a factual story well, you have to sort out the facts.
Below and on the next two pages is a picture story that you will be
writing about in this unit.

Exercise A

1. Examine the picture story carefully and make sure that you understand
   exactly what is going on.

2. Each picture is numbered. Write down the number of each picture and
   then write one sentence explaining what it shows.

3. You now have 15 sentences. Suppose you had to tell the whole story
   in just five sentences. How would you do it? Think carefully and then
   write five short sentences that tell the whole story.

Writing a report

Newspaper report

Now it is time to turn the picture story into a newspaper report. Stories in newspapers are organized in a special way. Journalists know that readers may not have time to read everything in the paper, so they make things easier for them. Look at the information below and then follow the instructions on the next page.

How a newspaper report is arranged

1. **Headline**
   This gives you some idea of what the story is about – and it may make a bit of a joke of it, as this one does.

2. **Lead paragraph**
   This tells you the most important thing in the story. It usually tries to make the reader want to find out more.

3. **Main story**
   This tells the story but without too many details.

4. **Details and background**
   For people who want to know more, this gives further information.

5. **Quotations**
   If the writer has interviewed people involved, there are quotations from what they said.

Pupils make a meal of it

PUPILS at Parr Community High School are learning about the most important meal of the day.

A breakfast club, funded by St Helen's College, sees Year 8 pupils working alongside their teachers to provide breakfast for their fellow pupils every Monday morning. They have also set up poster competitions and designed their own newsletter.

The aim is to encourage the children to work in teams, thus boosting their self-confidence and communication skills.

Malcolm Cowley, the careers adviser attached to the club, said: 'The secret of the club's success is that it is a partnership.'

'The school have supplied excellent facilities, we have had participation from interested adults from various agencies and the young people themselves have driven the club along with interest and enthusiasm.'

Writing a report

Exercise B

For this exercise you will need the sentences you wrote for Exercise A.

1. Look at the picture story again. How could you sum up the most important things about the story in just one or two sentences? Start by choosing two or three of these facts to concentrate on:

   - it happened at 4 in the morning
   - thousands of gallons of water poured into the house
   - a fireman was slightly injured
   - Mr Loftus was asleep
   - huge amounts of damage were done
   - Mr Loftus and his son had to leave their house.

   Write one or two sentences containing the facts you have chosen. This is your **lead paragraph**.

2. Now you are going to tell the **main story** in the order in which things happened. You are going to write one paragraph of no more than five sentences. Start by looking at your original list of five sentences. Use as many of them as you can and change or add to them as necessary.

3. Now it's time to think about the **details and background**. Look at the picture story again and the list of 15 sentences you wrote. Make a list of important details you want to include. Write one or two paragraphs about them. Don't write more than four sentences in each paragraph.

4. The picture story doesn't give us any **quotations**, so you will have to make them up. Make up two quotations:

   - what Mr Loftus said
   - what the fire chief said.

   Include each one in a paragraph which makes it clear who is speaking. Use the correct punctuation for direct speech (see page 137).

5. Finally you need a **headline**. Read through your story and think of a headline that:

   - sums up the story, and
   - makes people want to read it.

6. Now read through what you have written. Make sure that it makes sense and is clear and easy to understand. Make any changes needed. Correct any mistakes in spelling, punctuation and grammar.

Writing a report

More formal reports

You could write about the 'Pupils make a meal of it' story in a different way. St Helen's College is paying for the breakfast club in the story. If the principal of the college wanted to know how the money is being used, Malcolm Cowley might be asked to make a report.

The pattern of a formal report

1. **Title**
   This sums up what the report is about.

2. **Introduction**
   The first part tells us the most important facts.

3. **Body of the report**
   The main part of the report tells the story *in the order in which things happened*.

4. **Conclusion**
   The last part tells the reader the most important things about the subject. Here we read that the scheme is a success and we are told why this is so.

Parr Community High School Breakfast Club

The Breakfast Club was started at the beginning of the last school year and now has an active membership of 15. It regularly serves over 40 breakfasts every Monday morning.

At the beginning of September I held a meeting for all Year 8 pupils to explain the idea. Some were enthusiastic while others could not see the point of it. At the end of the meeting 30 students signed up to take part.

In the early stages there were not many customers for the breakfasts, but word soon got around that the breakfasts were good to eat and that people enjoyed themselves. By November we were regularly serving 20–30 meals.

This term active membership has dropped to 15, but these are all keen, enthusiastic students. The quality of the food has risen and so has the number of customers. The highest number we have had is 67, and the average this term has been 43.

The students are enthusiastic. They say that it has made them realize the importance of having a proper meal at the start of the day. We have also received good support from parents. The scheme is a great success.

Writing a report

Exercise C

The house in the story on pages 57–9 belongs to the local council. The result of the flood was that Mr Loftus and his son could no longer live in it. They had to ask the council to repair the damage and give them somewhere else to live until the repairs were finished. The council have asked Mr Loftus to write a short report explaining exactly what happened. It will have a total of five paragraphs:

1:	the introduction, summing up what has happened
2, 3 and 4:	the body of the report, describing what happened in the correct order
5:	the conclusion, explaining the effects of the flood and why Mr Loftus cannot live in the house at the moment.

For this exercise you will need the sentences you wrote for Exercise A.

Planning

1. Look at the picture story again. Now look at the fifteen sentences you wrote. Against each one, write:

   ✔ if it describes something the council should know
   ✘ if it describes something the council do not need to know.

2. Make a list of any other things you think the council should be told.

3. Now you are going to start planning your report. Begin with the **body of the report**. Use the answers you gave to questions 1 and 2 to help you decide what you will put in each of paragraphs 2, 3 and 4. Write a few words for each paragraph to remind you what you have decided.

Writing

4. Write paragraphs 2–4.

5. Now write the **introduction**. This needs to tell the council what the report is about and sum up in two or three sentences what happened. Altogether you should write no more than five sentences.

6. Finally write the **conclusion**.

Redrafting

7. You haven't written the report in the order people will read it in. You need to go through it and make changes so that it is clear and easy to follow. In particular, make sure that each paragraph leads on to the next, without a jump. Make any changes that are needed.

8. Write a clean final copy of the report.

Writing a report

Guidelines

Audience and purpose

It is always important to think about the kind of people who read reports and why they read them.

◆ Newspapers are read by many different people. They are mainly looking for:

- information
- entertainment.

Readers may have little or no knowledge about the story you are writing, so you often have to tell them everything right from the start. It is also a good idea to keep your sentences and vocabulary quite simple.

◆ More formal reports are read by fewer people. These readers usually have a special reason for reading a report: to get information. They may have some specialist knowledge of the subject, and you need to think about this. (For example, the local council know that Mr Loftus is a council tenant.)

Paragraphing

Make sure to read the section on writing paragraphs on page 25. All reports tell a story, so it is important to make sure that readers don't lose track of **when** things happened. Make sure that the **time links** between your sentences and paragraphs are clear. You can use words and phrases like:

then	earlier	later
at the beginning	in the end	the next day
in the morning	in the afternoon	finally

These are all **adverbials**. You can probably think of others you can use.

Sentence grammar

When you link clauses you will need to use **time conjunctions**. For example:

when	before	since	as	until	after	while

You need to make sure that you use the right **tense**. To tell the story you need to use **past tenses** (see page 112). To describe things that are still true, you need to use **present tenses** (see page 112).

Making a leaflet

Leaflets are used for many different purposes and are read by many different people.

In tests and exams you may be asked to write the text for a leaflet. This is a task that uses a lot of different skills and it can seem quite a daunting prospect when you start out. But like all writing tasks, it can be broken down into small, manageable sections. This unit shows you how to do this and then go on to write a successful leaflet.

On the next two pages there is a set of information (the *Datafile*) and pictures (the *Photofile*) about an imaginary outdoor holiday centre. Pages 68–71 then show you how to write a leaflet based on that material. Look at the material first and then work through pages 68–71.

Making a leaflet

Datafile

This is a set of notes that *Young Adventure UK* have given you for the leaflet.

ACTIVITIES

CANOEING — on our own private lake in holiday centre grounds – with 'rest area' + shop (soft drinks and snacks).
– also on R. Wart (1 km from centre) – for more experienced students.

SAILBOARDING – on lake. Tuition for beginners on 'dry land sailboard'. Coaching for more experienced.

ABSEILING — abseil wall and tower in grounds – training in safety and techniques.

MOUNTAIN BIKES – off-road course with 'thrills and spills' in centre grounds – also special forest and hill trails at nearby Lost Souls Peak – bikes and helmets provided.

QUAD BIKES – all the fun of off-road driving, but no danger – special course and tuition – all kids love it.

PONY TREKKING – long and short trails round Dark Forest and Low Peak – all tuition and kit provided.

STAFF AND SAFETY

TEAM STAFF – students work in small groups – each group has team staff 'mother' or 'father' in charge – go round with them on all activities – deal with problems.

ACTIVITY STAFF – each activity has specialist staff member in charge – trained in safety and first aid techniques.

TRAINING — all staff have training and safety certificates – all are hand picked.

ACCOMMODATION

ACTIVITY CENTRE – indoor activities + dining area and rest areas in beautiful 19th-century manor house set in own grounds.

DORMITORIES – specially designed 'log cabins' each for 4–6 boys or girls plus team staff member (sleeps on premises).

Making a leaflet

Photofile

You can choose from these photographs, or you can ask for particular photographs to be taken specially to illustrate your leaflet.

1

2

3

4

5

6

Making a leaflet

Before you write

The task

You have been asked to plan and write a leaflet advertising an outdoor holiday centre. *Young Adventure UK* offer activity courses for school parties during term time and for activity holidays for individual children during the school holidays. The children are all aged 9–13.

This leaflet is to be read by parents who might send their children on one of the holidays. It has to show them how exciting and enjoyable the holidays are, but it must also reassure the parents. They need to feel confident that their children will be safe and well cared for.

Planning

The leaflet is to be a single sheet of A4, folded once to make four pages:

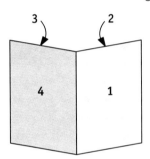

Begin by planning what you will put on each of the four pages.

Page 1: This is the front of the leaflet. It will have a big picture of the holiday centre and an introduction telling readers what a splendid place it is. *This has already been written, so you don't need to do anything.*

Pages 2 and 3: This is what people see when they open the leaflet out. It contains these things:

◆ information about activities
◆ pictures of activities, with captions.

Page 4: This is the back of the leaflet. It contains:

◆ information about accommodation at the holiday centre
◆ information about the staff
◆ information about safety.

Making a leaflet

1. Prepare pages 2–3. You are going to write four or five paragraphs (two or three on each page). You can use up to three photographs. Decide what will go in each paragraph. Write a few words for each to remind you what you have decided. Write the numbers of the photographs you have chosen. If you want special photographs write a description of what will be in them.

2. Prepare page 4. You are going to write three paragraphs. You can use one photograph. Decide what will go in each paragraph. Write a few words for each to remind you what you have decided. Write the number of the photograph you have chosen. If you want a special photograph to be taken, write a description of what will be in it.

Drafting

3. Now write the first draft of the paragraphs you have planned. As you write, remember:
   • your audience is the mothers and fathers of children aged 9–13
   • your purpose is to persuade them that the adventure holidays are exciting, enjoyable – and safe.

4. Try to keep each paragraph short: not more than five sentences in each. Keep your sentences fairly short, too.

5. When you have finished writing, either:
   • get someone else to read your first draft and comment on it, or
   • leave a gap of time before reading it through yourself.

6. Check that your writing:
   • is clear
   • talks directly to your audience
   • carries out your purpose
   • fits in with your planned illustrations.

   Make any necessary changes.

Presentation

How you present your writing depends on how you are going to put the words on paper:

◆ handwriting

◆ using a computer and a word-processing program

◆ using a computer and a page layout (DTP) program.

Making a leaflet

7. Handwriting

Take a sheet of paper and draw left and right margins in pencil about 9 cm apart. Write out your paragraphs between these margins. Leave a space between the paragraphs. Write neatly and as small as you can – but it must be readable! When you have finished, rub out the margins.

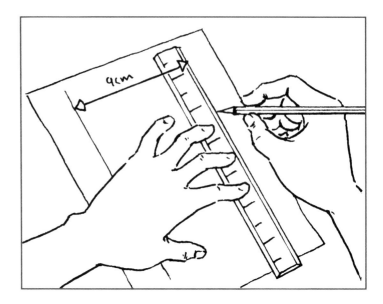

Using a word processor

Set the page margins to 9cm apart. Make the letter sizes a bit larger than normal for ordinary text (say, 14 point). Key in your paragraphs, leaving spaces between them.

Now follow instructions 8 and 9 for 'Handwriting'.

Using a page layout program

Work on A4 turned sideways ('landscape'), with two pages on each sheet:

Page 4	Page 1

Page 2	Page 3

(Remember that you don't have to write page 1.)

8. Handwriting

Cut each paragraph out separately.

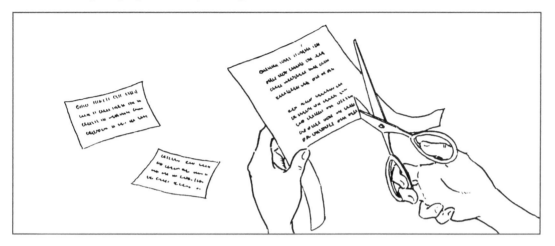

Using a page layout program

Do a rough layout of the boxes for each of your paragraphs, and for each of your illustrations.

9. Handwriting

Handwriting is usually quite a bit bigger than print, so use a separate sheet of A4 for each of the three pages of the leaflet, rather than the folded sheet of A4. Arrange the paragraphs and spaces for the pictures on each page of the leaflet. Draw rectangles where the pictures will go. Stick down the paragraphs in the right places. Write captions describing what is in each photograph. Give each page a heading – and any sub-headings you think will be useful.

Using a page layout program

Key in your paragraphs. Re-size the text boxes as necessary and rearrange each page as necessary.

10. Using a page layout program

Key in a caption for each of the picture boxes, describing what is in it.

Writing an article

Articles can be read in many different publications. In this unit you will be looking at feature articles written for entertainment and for information.

◆ Do you enjoy reading feature articles?

◆ What kind of articles do you read?

◆ In which magazines or newspapers do you read them?

◆ What do you look for in a feature article?

This unit shows you how to write a feature article.

Writing an article

Choosing a subject

Begin by thinking about the subject of your article.

What kind of subject?

Writers choose many different subjects, but common ones are:

◆ famous (or not-so-famous) people

◆ sports and outdoor activities

◆ travel and interesting places

◆ lifestyle (clothes, fashion, make-up, food, interior decor)

◆ pop music – songs, singers, bands

◆ film and TV

◆ gardening, DIY

◆ hobbies and leisure interests.

> 1 Are chimps like humans?
> 2 A holiday in Brittany
> 3 Racing BMX bikes

When you have thought about this, make a short list of subjects you could write about. As you go through the next stages you will have to cut this list down to one – the subject you are going to write about.

Thinking about the audience

Now think about your audience. For each of the subjects on your list, write short answers to these four questions:

1 What kind of reader will be interested in an article about each of these subjects?

2 How easy or hard will it be to make the subject interesting for them?

3 How much will they already know about the subject? (So how much explaining will you have to do?)

4 What kind of newspaper or magazine will the article appear in?

> Are chimps like humans?
> 1 People are interested in animals
> 2 Not very difficult – as long as it's not too complicated
> 3 Not much
> 4 Wildlife magazine

Writing an article

Doing your research

How do you know about this subject?

Very often articles are based on one of these:

◆ **a personal experience**

In this case all you need do is remember everything clearly and possibly make some notes about what you remember.

◆ **a special interest that you know a lot about**

Again, you probably have most of the information you need, but you may also need to look some things up.

◆ **a subject you think is interesting**

In this case you may know something about the subject, but will also have to do some research about the subject.

For each of the subjects on your list, think about where your information will come from. Make short notes about this.

> Are chimps like humans?
> _ know some of it
> - look the rest up in wildlife books (library) and magazine (at home)

At this point you need to decide which of the subjects in your list you are going to write about.

Making notes

Now make notes:

◆ what you already know

◆ based on the books and magazines you have consulted.

Writing an article

If you can find any pictures to copy or cut out, add these
to your notes.

Are chimps 'just like us'?

Using tools

- Chimpanzees like eating ants
- Poke stick into ants' nest to get ants out
- some have learned to use longer stick – leave
  it in nest longer – get more ants out – push
  ants into mouth with other hand

Dancing

- Traditional societies celebrate arrival of
  rains (important for farmers) with singing
  and dancing
- Chimpanzees celebrate a downpour of rain by dancing
- Not an instinct – the children learn it from their parents

DNA

- Humans and chimpanzees had same ancestors 5 million years ago
- Scientists have compared DNA of humans and chimpanzees (DNA
  is the biological 'code' that makes us as we are)
- Our DNA is 98% the same
- We've got more in common with chimpanzees than African
  elephants have with Indian elephants

Language

- Humans use language, animals don't
- Captive chimps can be taught sign language
- Communicate with humans looking after them
- Even use it to communicate with each other when the humans
  aren't there

Sorting pictures

- Tame chimpanzees think they're human
- One young chimpanzee brought up with human family
- Sorting photographs into 'human'/'animal'
- Found picture of self – put in 'human' pile
- Found picture of father – put in 'animal' pile

Writing an article

Making a plan

Before you can start to write the article, you need to sort out the material you have collected. To do this, you need to make a plan.

1. Look at the notes you have made. Look for a pattern so that you can tell your readers about the subject in a way they will understand.

2. Make a list of the main points you want to cover. (Don't worry at the moment about how the article will begin and end.)

> Are chimps like humans?
> 1 DNA
> 2 Using tools
> 3 Sign language
> 4 Sorting Photos

Writing the first draft

1. Before you start to write, leave a space of 12 lines at the beginning. This is for the first paragraph. You will write this after you have finished the rest of the article.

2. When you write, only use every other line – to leave space for revisions.

3. Now write the main part of your article. Write one or two paragraphs for each of the main points in your list.

Revising and completing

1. When you have finished the main part, leave it, if possible, and do something else.

2. After a break read it through and make any changes you need – use the blank lines you left.

3. As you revise, think about how to begin the article. Try to think of something that will 'grab' the reader's attention.

4. Write a short 'attention-grabbing' paragraph at the beginning of your article.

5. Look at the last paragraph. Think of a way of rounding the article off. Write a short concluding paragraph.

Writing an article

Guidelines

Audience and purpose

As you have seen, there are magazine and newspaper articles for every different kind of reader. So you need to think carefully about your readers:

◆ **Are they reading just to be generally informed and entertained, or have they got a special interest?**
This will tell you how much background information you need to give them and how much you can take it for granted that they know 'the basics' of the subject.

◆ **How can I catch their interest and then keep it as they read the article?**
Although feature articles are based on information, many people read them mainly to be entertained. If they don't enjoy reading your article, they will stop before the end.

Paragraphing

Make sure to read the section on writing paragraphs on page 25.

◆ When you plan a feature article you should 'think in paragraphs': make a list of the main points you want to cover and give each point one or two paragraphs when you write. (If you find you need more than two, you are probably covering more than one main point.)

◆ If possible, don't write the first and last paragraphs until you have finished the main part of the article *and revised it*. This will give you a much better idea of what the whole article is like and so how to begin and end it.

Sentence grammar

A good article 'flows' easily from one point to the next. One good way of doing this is to make sure that you use **sentence adverbials** well. For example:

as a result	interestingly	in spite of this
on the other hand	to everyone's surprise	even so

Vocabulary

One of the big differences between good writing and bad writing is in the *choice of words*. Compare these two short texts:

A

On Wednesday we <u>went</u> to see my gran. We <u>went</u> on the bus to Parsons Road Station, then we <u>went</u> on a train to Lydham. After that we <u>went</u> in a taxi to her house ...

B

On Wednesday we <u>visited</u> my gran. We <u>caught</u> the bus to Parsons Road Station, then we <u>travelled</u> by train to Lydham. After that we <u>took</u> a taxi to her house ...

Text A quickly becomes boring because the writer repeats the same word, 'went', several times. B is much more interesting because it uses four different words: 'visited', 'caught', 'travelled' and 'took'.

The number of words you know is called your **vocabulary**. The writer of B shows a bigger vocabulary than the writer of A. In fact we all have two different vocabularies:

◆ words we know well and use when we speak or write

◆ words we recognize and understand but don't normally use.

You can try this for yourself. The list of words below comes from the same page of a dictionary. Write the words out in three groups:

1. words you know and use

2. words you recognize and think you understand but wouldn't normally use

3. words you don't know.

Words		
doughty	downcast	doze
dour	downpour	dozen
dove	downright	drab
dovetail	downstairs	draconian
dowdy	downtrodden	draft
down-and-out	downturn	
downbeat	doyen	

Vocabulary

Increasing your vocabulary

Most people know far more words than they ever use. One way of becoming a better writer is to use more words – and that means trying out some of those words that you know but never use. There are two tools you can use to help you:

◆ dictionary   ◆ thesaurus.

Using a dictionary

Dictionaries provide a lot of useful information.

headword: this is the main word for that set of definitions. Any other words included are based on the headword.

definition: an explanation of the meaning of the word or phrase.

usage: examples of how the word is used, to give you a clearer idea of its meaning. This is particularly useful if the word has more than one meaning.

pronunciation: some dictionaries use ordinary letters. Others use a special alphabet.

adjoin

adjoins the balcony'.
[AD- + Latin *jungere* to join]

adjourn (*say* **a-jern**) *verb*
to break off or postpone: 'the meeting was *adjourned* until the next day'.
Word Family: **adjournment**, *noun*, a) the act of adjourning, b) the state or time of being adjourned.
[AD- + Latin *diurnus* daily]

adjudicate (*say* **a-joodi-kate**) *verb*
to judge or settle a dispute, etc.
Word Family: **adjud**ication, *noun*; adju-
dicator, *noun*, a pers

word class: this helps you know how the word can be used.

adjunct (*say* **ajjunkt**) *n*
something added or i
[Latin *adjunctum* som

adjure (*say* **a-joor**) *verb*
to solemnly command or request.

related words: if there are other words in the word family these are grouped together here.

juration, *noun*.
are to swear]

verb
hape, form or position of something, so that it fits.
2. to change oneself to match the circumstances: 'it is hard to *adjust* to a new way of life'.
Word Family: **adjustment**, *noun*; **adjustable**, *adjective*.

Vocabulary

Finding the right word

If you know what you want to say but can't quite think of the word to use, a dictionary is not much use. What you need is a thesaurus. Suppose, for example, you are looking for another word for 'worried', a thesaurus might give you:

troubled	concerned	caring	anxious	fretting
harassed	haunted	tormented	disturbed	agitated
upset	distressed	unsettled	uncomfortable	

Choosing the right word

Then you have the problem of deciding which one to use! Some words are just not suitable for some audiences. For example, which of these words and phrases would you use when talking to your headteacher?

troubled	in a funk	on edge
freaked out	concerned	in a cold sweat

Sometimes the choice is more difficult. You need to choose the words that have the right *strength*. Suppose you are writing about being worried because you have lost your key to get into the house. You could use any of the words in the list at the top of the page. But some of them are not suitable. If you said you were 'uncomfortable' it sounds a bit feeble, but to describe yourself as 'tormented' is almost certainly too much. Words of a similar meaning can often be organized into a kind of league table, according to their strength:

tormented
distressed

↓

anxious
uncomfortable

tormented   uncomfortable

Get into the habit of thinking about words in this way and it will help you when you have to make choices as a writer.

Vocabulary

Exercise A

Each of the words in this group has a similar meaning, but some are stronger than others. Put them into a league table with the strongest at the top.

cheerful	contented	delighted	happy
joyful	pleased	starry-eyed	thrilled

Now do the same for these two groups of words:

downhearted	glum	grief-stricken	miserable
sad	suicidal	tearful	unhappy
arrogant	big-headed	conceited	proud
self-important	self-satisfied	swanky	vain

Word families

You may have noticed that some words seem to be linked together in 'families'. For example, if you were asked to think of all the words that contained the letters 'appear', you might come up with:

appear	appearance	disappear
reappear	disappearance	reappearance

We can arrange these words in another way:

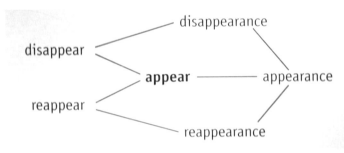

These words are all made up by adding groups of letters before and after *appear*:

PREFIX	STEM	SUFFIX
dis		
	appear	ance
re		

Vocabulary

Exercise B

Make similar word family diagrams for each of these groups of words:

climb	over-sharp	foresee	mark
climbable	sharp	foreseeable	markable
unclimbable	sharpen	foreseen	marked
unclimbed	sharpener	see	remark
	sharpish	seeable	remarkable
	unsharp	seen	unmarkable
		unforeseeable	unmarked
		unforeseen	unremarkable
		unseen	

Parts of a word

Stem

appear is the stem of all the words we listed in the diagram on page 81. Some words only have a stem. Examples are:

> appear   door   happy   green

Prefix

Groups of letters that come before the stem are called **prefixes**. They are 'fixed' before ('pre') the stem. Prefixes change the meaning of the stem in some way. So if we add 'dis-' to *appear,* we make a word that has the opposite meaning. 'Re-' means 'again'. Look at the table of common prefixes on page 83.

Exercise C

In the table below there are five prefixes and 15 stems. You can use them to make 15 words. You should use each prefix three times and each stem once.

anti-	aircraft	espionage	pilot
auto-	attack	feminist	social
counter-	behave	graph	spell
mid-	biography	night	summer
mis-	carry	offensive	way

Vocabulary

Common prefixes

Prefix	Meaning	Examples
anti-	against	anti-poverty
arch-	chief	archbishop
auto-	self	autograph
bi-	two	bicycle
co-	joint, together	co-operate
counter-	against	counter-attack
de-	making the opposite of	de-ice
dis-	making the opposite of	disappear
ex-	former	ex-miner
	out of	extract
fore-	in the front of, ahead of	foreground
hyper-	very big	hypermarket
in-	not, opposite of	inhuman
	in, into	inshore
inter-	between	inter-party
mega-	very large	megaphone
mid-	middle	midweek
mini-	small	minidisc
mis-	wrong, false	mislead
mono-	one	monocycle
multi-	many	multi-coloured
non-	not, opposite of	non-fiction
out-	beyond	outspoken
over-	too much	overboard
post-	after	post-examination
pre-	before	pre-school
pro-	for	pro-health
re-	again	rewrite
	back	repay
self-	self	self-aware
semi-	half	semi-darkness
sub-	below	submarine
super-	more than, special	supersonic
tele-	at a distance	television
trans-	across	transworld
tri-	three	triplets
un-	not, opposite of	unhelpful
under-	below, less than	underweight

Vocabulary

Suffix

Groups of letters that come after the stem are called **suffixes**. Suffixes don't change the meaning of the word, they change the way in which we can use it. For example:

appear = verb
*(In spring the first flowers **appear**.)*

appearance = noun
*(After the **appearance** of the swallows we know summer is on the way.)*

Common suffixes

Making verbs

| -en | deaden |
| -ize | modernize |

Making nouns

-ation	exploration
-er	walker
-ist	violinist
-ity	regularity
-ment	arrangement
-ness	kindness
-or	actor

Making adjectives

-able	washable
-ful	helpful
-ish	childish
-ive	attractive
-less	careless
-like	childlike
-ly	cowardly
-y	hairy

Making adverbs

-ly	calmly
-wards	homewards
-wise	clockwise

Exercise D

Think of two words that end with each of the following suffixes:

-ize   -ation   -ment   -able   -less

Spelling

Some people find spelling much harder than others. But even if you seem to be always making spelling mistakes there are things you can do:

1. **Work out what your problem words are.**
   Go back through your writing and check which words have been corrected. Make a list of mistakes that you repeat.

2. **Keep a spelling notebook.**
   Write down – correctly! – all your problem words. When you look up new words you want to use, write them down.

3. **Always use a dictionary when you write.**

4. **Look – cover – spell – write – check.**
   If you have problems with a word:

   - look carefully at how it is spelled
   - cover it over
   - spell it out in your head
   - write it down (without looking at it again)
   - check that it is right.

5. **Learn the rules for patterns and changes.**
   These come next in this unit.

6. **Learn the lists of common words which have double letters in them.**
   These come later in this unit.

7. **Learn the words that are easily confused.**
   These come at the end of this unit.

Spelling

Spelling patterns

'i' before 'e' except after 'c'

This rule only works when the sound the letters 'ie' and 'ei' make is the long 'ee' sound you hear in 'sweet'.

Examples of 'ie': thief, grief
Examples of 'ei': receive, deceit
Exceptions: counterfeit, protein, seize, either, neither, species.

'c' or 's'?

Is it 'practice' or 'practise'? The rule is simple:

'c' for a noun, and 's' for a verb

You can remember this because the letters C – N – S – V (**C** = **N**oun, **S** = **V**erb) are in alphabetical order. For example:

NOUN	VERB
practice	practise
licence	license
prophecy	prophesy

'-ise' or '-ize'?

This is a rule that is changing – and some words can be spelled either way. You will never be wrong if you follow this rule: always use '-ise', except for 'capsize'.

'-able' or '-ible'?

This is more difficult. This is a list of the commonest words that end in '-ible':

accessible	audible	collapsible	credible
digestible	divisible	edible	flexible
horrible	incredible	invisible	illegible
irresistible	possible	responsible	sensible
terrible	visible		

The chances are that if the word you want to use isn't in that list, it ends with '-able'. Usually with words that end in '-able' you can remove the '-able' and you will still be left with a complete word. For example:

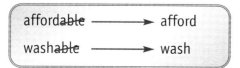

affordable ⟶ afford
washable ⟶ wash

If in doubt, look the word up in a dictionary.

Spelling

Exercise A

Write out each of the following words, putting in the missing letters:

1. c_ _ling
2. ch_ _f
3. collaps_ble
4. conc_ _ve
5. dec_ _ve
6. horr_ble
7. incred_ble
8. n_ _ther

9. p_ _ce
10. prot_ _n
11. rel_ _f
12. s_ _ze
13. understand_ble
14. unrepeat_ble
15. vis_ble

Rules based on changes

Adding '-s'

When you make a noun into a plural you usually have to add an 's'. When you use verbs in the present tense you often have to add an 's'. The rules for both are the same:

1. Normally just add '-s': *book   books*

2. Add '-es' to words that end in '-ch', '-s', '-sh', '-x' or '-z': *matches, bosses, rushes, taxes, buzzes*

3. If a word ends in '-f' or '-fe', remove the ending and add '-ves':

   thief   thieves   life   lives

   Exceptions: *beliefs, chiefs, dwarfs, griefs, proofs, roofs*

4. If a word ends with a consonant followed by '-y', change the 'y' to 'ies':
   cry   cries

5. If a word ends in '-o', add '-s', except for:

buffaloes	dominoes	echoes	goes
grottoes	haloes	heroes	mangoes
mosquitoes	potatoes	tomatoes	tornadoes
torpedoes	volcanoes		

Spelling

Exercise B

Write down the plural of each of the following words:

1. belief
2. boss
3. bunch
4. bush
5. child

6. copy
7. genius
8. goose
9. lilo
10. ray

11. roof
12. sheep
13. taxi
14. tomato
15. woman

Adding '-ed' and '-ing'

When you use a verb, you often have to change the spelling:

I walk   *I walk**ed***   *I am walk**ing***

Sometimes you have to change the way the rest of the word is spelled too. Often you can just add '-ed' and '-ing', but there are a lot of exceptions. These are the main rules:

1. If the verb ends in a consonant followed by '-y', change the 'y' to an 'i' before adding '-ed':

   deny   *denied*

2. **Words of only one syllable**

   If the vowel is short (like the vowels in these words: *tap, bet*) and the word ends with a single consonant, you double the consonant:

   tap   *tapped, tapping*
   bet   *betted, betting*

   If the vowel is long and the word ends in '-e' (like the vowel sounds in these words: *hate, hope*), you remove the final '-e':

   hate   *hated, hating*
   hope   *hoped, hoping*

   But: if the '-e' comes after another vowel, add '-d' and '-ing':

   hoe   *hoed, hoeing*

3. **Words of more than one syllable that end with a single consonant**

   If the stress is on the last syllable, double the consonant:

   repel   *repelled, repelling*

   If the stress is not on the last syllable, just add '-ed' and '-ing':

   benefit   *benefited, benefiting*

Spelling

Exercise C

Copy and complete the following table. Be careful, there's at least one trap!

walk	walking	walked
beg		
compel		
dare		
fray		
lay		
mope		
pat		
pay		
peel		
put		
rake		
say		
sharpen		
smile		
spy		

Adding '-ly'

Adjectives can often be made into adverbs by adding '-ly':

quick   *quickly*

But there are these exceptions:

1. If the word ends in '-ll', just add '-y':

dull   *dully*

2. If the word has more than one syllable and ends in '-y', change the 'y' to 'i':

crazy   *crazily*

3. If the word has one syllable ending in '-y' , just add '-ly', except for:

daily, gaily

4. If the word ends with a consonant followed by '-le', remove the '-e' and add '-y':

horrible   *horribly*

Spelling

Adding '-er' and '-est'

The comparative and superlative of many short adjectives are made by adding '-er' and '-est':

tall ⟶ *taller* ⟶ *tallest*

But there are these exceptions:

1. If the word ends with a consonant followed by '-y', change the 'y' to 'i':

crazy ⟶ *crazier* ⟶ *craziest*

2. If the word has one syllable and a long vowel sound, and ends in '-e', remove the 'e':

tame ⟶ *tamer* ⟶ *tamest*

3. If the word has one syllable and a short vowel sound, and ends with a single consonant, double the last consonant:

mad ⟶ *madder* ⟶ *maddest*

4. If the word ends in '-l', add '-er' and '-est'.

There is one exception: *cruel* ⟶ *crueller* ⟶ *cruellest*

Double letters

It is easy to put double letters where there should only be one and to miss out one of a pair of double letters. The best thing is to learn the problem words in groups.

No double letters

Some words sound as if they should have double letters but have none! The commonest are:

fulfil	imitate	marvel	omit
patrol	pedal	transmit	

One pair of double letters

The commonest are:

accelerate	accident	accurate	assist
beginning	brilliant	caterpillar	collapse
collect	commemorate	commit	corridor
disappear	disappoint	dissatisfied	discuss
exaggerate	excellent	gorilla	happen(ed)
harass	illustrate	immediate	millionaire
necessary	occasion	occur	parallel
proceed	procession	professional	scissors
sheriff	succeed	sufficient	terrible
tomorrow			

Two pairs of double letters

The commonest are:

accommodation	accidentally	address	commission
committed	embarrass	guerrilla	happiness
mattress	millennium	possess	successful
unnecessary	woollen		

Spelling

Words that can be confused

accept/except	If you **accept** something, you receive it from someone else. We use **except** to mean that something has been left out: 'Everyone **except** James ...'
bail/bale	You **bail** out a boat (and people who are arrested apply for **bail**). A **bale** is a bundle of straw or paper.
buy/by/bye	You **buy** things at the shops. **By** is a preposition: 'It was given to me **by** my sister.' In a knockout competition, if you get a **bye** you go through into the next round without having to compete.
curb/kerb	If you **curb** something, you hold it back. The **kerb** is what runs along a pavement or road.
currant/current	**Currants** are dried fruit. You find **currents** in seas and rivers.
lead/led	**Lead** can be pronounced 'leed' or 'led'. The first word means the thing you put on a dog to stop it running away. The second is a heavy metal. **Led** is the past form of 'to lead'.
loose/lose	If a dog is **loose** it is not tied up. If you **lose** something, you cannot find it.
miner/minor	A **miner** digs for coal and other minerals. A **minor** is someone who is under-age.
passed/past	**Passed** comes from the verb 'to pass', in sentences like 'I've **passed** my exams.' **Past** is a preposition ('Our house is just **past** the corner') or an adjective ('He is a **past** master of it').
sight/site	A **sight** is something you see. A **site** is the place where something happens – for example, a building site.
stationary/stationery	If a car is **stationary** it is not moving. **Stationery** is paper, envelopes and other things you might buy at a stationer's. (Remember it by: '**E** for **e**nvelopes, **A** for c**a**rs.')
to/too/two	It is all **too** easy **to** confuse these words even when you see **two** of them side by side.

Spelling

Exercise D

Each of the following sentences contains one or two blanks. After each blank there are a number of possible spellings of the word that should go in the blank. Write down the correct spelling of each word.

1. 'I'm really bored,' she said _____ (duly/dully/dullly).

2. I don't like people who _____ (immitate/imitate) the way I speak.

3. I last saw Pat sitting on the _____ (cerb/curb/kerb/kurb).

4. I was just about to eat the apple when I saw there was a _____ (catarpiller/caterpilar/caterpillar) on it.

5. I'm not allowed to vote because I'm a _____ (miner/minor).

6. It's cruel to leave dogs alone at home but it's even _____ (crueler/crueller) to shut them in a car on a hot day.

7. Jean seems even _____ (crazier/crazyer) than last time I met her.

8. That is the _____ (saddest/sadest) film I've ever seen.

9. That's the kind of situation that really _____ (embarases/embarasses/embarrases/embarrasses) me.

10. We needed paper, so we went to a _____ (stationary/stationery) shop.

11. We rang the hotel to see if there was any _____ (acomodation/accomodation/acommodation/accommodation) available.

12. We're travelling to Scotland by bike. We shall rely entirely on _____ (peddle/peddal/pedal) power.

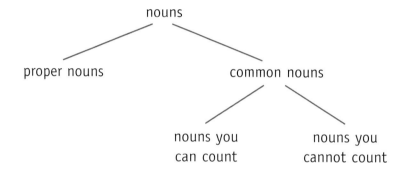

Word classes

Nouns

What is a noun?

Most nouns tell us about people, places, things and ideas. They:

◆ often have a plural (one **table**, two **tables**)

◆ can usually have words like *a, an, the* and *some* in front of them
(*a* **table**, *the* **tables**)

◆ can usually have adjectives in front of them (*the* *blue* **table**).

How do we use nouns?

Nouns can be divided into groups. The nouns in each group are used in
slightly different ways:

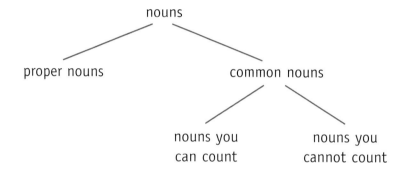

Proper nouns

These are the names of people, places, and things that are special.
Usually there is only one of them. For example:

William Shakespeare   London

As you can see, proper nouns are written starting with a capital letter.

Common nouns

All nouns that are not proper nouns are called common nouns. Common
nouns do not start with a capital letter, unless they come at the
beginning of a sentence. They can be divided into nouns that can be
counted and nouns that cannot be counted.

Word classes

Nouns that cannot be counted

Some nouns do not have a plural because they tell us about things that cannot be counted. For example:

butter   mud   excitement   weather

Nouns that can be counted

Most nouns can be counted. They have a plural. This is usually made by adding '-s' or '-es' (see spelling rules on page 87). Other plurals are made in different ways:

books   branches   children   sheep

Noun guidelines

Nouns shouldn't cause you many problems when you write, except for:

◆ **the correct spelling of plurals**

This is explained in detail on page 87.

◆ **nouns that can be counted**

You should not use these words before them:

little   less   least

Instead you should use:

few   fewer   fewest

So you should write *less butter* but *fewer plates*.

Exercise A

Divide the following nouns into three groups:

◆ proper nouns
◆ common nouns that can be counted
◆ common nouns that cannot be counted.

Note: the proper nouns should begin with capital letters, but they don't in this text.

1. sand
2. excitement
3. samuel
4. shoe
5. italy

6. shakespeare
7. television
8. pen
9. sadness
10. rubbish

Word classes

Adjectives

What is an adjective?

Adjectives work with nouns and some verbs to answer these questions:

◆ What kind of thing is it?   ◆ What is it like?

The adjectives in these sentences are in **bold** type:

> The **tropical** plants in the greenhouse include bananas.
> Your tea is **ready**.

How do we use adjectives?

Adjectives are used in two ways:

◆ **with nouns**
   They usually come before the noun. We say they **modify** the noun:
   A large grey wooden door

◆ **after verbs like 'to be'**
   The door was grey.

Different kinds of adjective

We can put adjectives into two groups:

1 adjectives that tell us what things are like – for example:
   green   happy   tiny   stupid

2 adjectives that put things into groups or classes – for example:
   annual   unique

Grading adjectives

Adjectives can be **graded**. You can put a word (an **adverb**) in front of them, as follows:

> A bright student
> A **fairly** bright student
> A **very** bright student

Fairly takes away from the meaning of *bright*, but *very* adds to it. You can also compare things using adjectives:

> Peter is **bright**.
> Jane is **brighter** than Peter.
> Mark is the **brightest** student in the class.

Brighter is called the **comparative** form, and *brightest* is the **superlative** form. If the adjective has more than two syllables, then you don't add '-er' or '-est', but use 'more' and 'most' instead:

> Peter is **intelligent**.
> Jane is **more intelligent** than Peter.
> Mark is the **most intelligent** student in the class.

Word classes

Adjective guidelines

Adjectives don't cause many problems for writers. Two things to remember are:

◆ You use the **comparative** when you are comparing two things. You can't use the **superlative** unless there are at least three. So it is wrong to say:

*Between Dave and Sam, Dave is by far the **cleverest**.*

You must say:

*Between Dave and Sam, Dave is by far the **cleverer**.*

◆ You can **grade** most adjectives, but not all of them. As we saw earlier, some adjectives answer the question 'What kind of thing?' They do this by putting the noun into a group or class:

*an **annual** event   a **unique** occasion*

You can't put words like *very* and *fairly* before this kind of adjective. So it is wrong to call something *very unique*.

Verbs

Verbs need careful handling!

What is a verb?

We use verbs in sentences to talk about:

◆ **actions**

*The dog **ate** my homework.*

◆ **states**

*Jim **slept** all the way through the maths lesson.*

There are also verbs that **link** the subject and the rest of the sentence:

*Jim **was** happy.*

There is more about linking verbs on page 122.

A verb can stand alone as the verb of a sentence, or it can be part of the verb phrase. This is explained in detail on pages 111–12.

How do we use verbs?

There are three kinds of verb:

1. main verbs

- These are verbs that can stand alone as the verb in a sentence:
  *The dog **ate** my homework.*
  *The teacher **shouted** at me.*

- If you look up a main verb in a dictionary you will find an explanation of what it means.

Word classes

2. auxiliary verbs

- These are verbs which are used with main verbs to make a verb phrase.

- They are:

> to be (is, was, were, etc.)
> to have (have, had, etc.)
> to do (do, did, etc.)

plus:

> may, might, can, could, will, would, shall, should, must

3. be, have, do

These three verbs can be used as auxiliaries: *I **have done** my homework.*

They can also be used as main verbs: *We **have** a lot of homework tonight.*

Changing the form of the verb

When we use a verb in a sentence, we may have to change its form. Look at the verb in each of these sentences:

> Jane **walks** to school every morning.
> Jane was **walking** to school yesterday and **walked** into a lamppost.
> She has **walked** with a limp ever since.
> She is going to **walk** more carefully from now on.

Verbs have these five forms:

1 **present tense forms:** walk/walks 2 **past tense form:** walked
3 **present participle:** walking 4 **past participle:** walked
5 **infinitive:** to walk

These five forms are all made from the **stem**: walk. Most verbs follow the same pattern, but some of the commonest verbs do not. These are called **irregular** verbs:

stem	present tense	present participle	past tense	past participle	infinitive
be	am/is/are	being	was/were	been	to be
have	has/have	having	had	had	to have
do	do/does	doing	did	done	to do
go	go/goes	going	went	gone	to go
swim	swim/swims	swimming	swam	swum	to swim
get	get/gets	getting	got	got	to get

Word classes

Exercise B

1. Divide the following verbs into two groups:

   ◆ main verbs
   ◆ auxiliary verbs.

1	can	6	must
2	could	7	perform
3	expect	8	should
4	hit	9	sing
5	may	10	walk

2. Copy and complete the following table:

stem	present tense	present participle	past tense	past participle	infinitive
burst buy cut find see sew show speak swell swing					

Word classes

Adverbs

What is an adverb?

Adverbs are used with:

◆ **verbs**
*She <u>swam</u> **slowly**.*

◆ **adjectives**
*Her swimming was **really** <u>slow</u>.*

◆ **adverbs**
*She swam **extremely** <u>slowly</u>.*

◆ **whole sentences**
***Fortunately** <u>no one was waiting for her</u>.*

As you can see, many adverbs are formed by adding '-ly' to an adjective. But many very common adverbs are not formed in this way. For example:

> well   backwards   often

Another way of picking out adverbs is that very many of them answer one of these four questions:

◆ **Where?**
*She fell **down**.*

◆ **When?**
*I'll do it **later**.*

◆ **How?**
*She cycled **energetically** up the hill.*

◆ **How much?**
*That coat is **incredibly** expensive.*

Word classes

How do we use adverbs?

As we saw on page 100, sometimes an adverb works with a single word, like a verb, an adjective, or another adverb. If so it is often placed very close, either just after the verb:

*She <u>swam</u> **slowly**.*

or just before an adjective or adverb:

*... **really** <u>slow</u>   ... **extremely** <u>slowly</u> ...*

Adverbs that tell us about the whole sentence can be used in a number of different ways. They may answer the questions 'Where?', 'When?' and 'How?'. On the other hand they may do two other important jobs:

◆ **showing the link between two sentences**

*I was wearing a raincoat. **Therefore** I stayed dry and warm.*

◆ **making a comment on something you've just said**

*I was wearing a raincoat. **Surprisingly** I still got soaked.*

Sentence adverbs can come in different places:

> **Probably** it was because she was eating all the time.
> It was **probably** because she was eating all the time.
> It was because she was eating all the time, **probably**.

Adverb guidelines

The biggest problem you're likely to face when you use adverbs is deciding where to put them in the sentence. Each of these sentences means something different:

> 1 **Only** the teachers are worried about John's exam results.
>
> 2 The teachers are **only** worried about John's exam results.
>
> 3 The teachers are worried about **only** John's exam results.

Sentence 1 means that no one else is worried. Sentence 2 means that the exam results are the only thing they are worried about. Sentence 3 means that they aren't worried about any one else's exam results. So be careful where you put adverbs like 'only' and 'even'!

Also watch out for spelling problems when you add '-ly' to an adjective to turn it into an adverb. Look on page 89 for the rules.

Word classes

Exercise C

There are 13 adverbs in the following text. Pick them out and write them down (some have been used more than once).

It's not easy being a boy. Being a boy is tough because, even from a very early age, a great deal is expected of you. Dads want you to play for your national football team, and they don't give up, do they? Oh, no. And if you're the firstborn, it's even worse. You get the old Son and Heir bit. They expect you to grow up and discover a cure for cancer while heading in a particularly tricky pass from Paul Gascoigne in a last-minute bid to clinch the match against Argentina in the World Cup which this year is taking place at the summit of a polar ice-cap for some strange reason. Merciful Heavens! Do those stupid parents of yours realize just how much skill and dexterity goes into getting your forehead to an ice-covered match ball when you're dressed in full arctic gear?

And what do these same devoted but ambitious parents expect of your sister? Nothing as long as she marries a nice bloke. Preferably one called Keith, who is either (a) capable of discovering a cure for cancer while heading in a particularly tricky pass from Paul Gascoigne in a last-minute etc., etc., or (b) a double-glazing salesman.

It's just not fair, is it? But then, there's nothing in the rules of life that says anything about it being fair. And Lord knows I've looked often enough! You'll just have to grin and bear it. Preferably a stupid inane grin that will convince your parents you're irretrievably insane and should be left well alone.

Word classes

Pronouns

What is a pronoun?

Pronouns 'stand in for' nouns and other parts of the sentence, so that we don't have to keep on repeating ourselves.

Personal pronouns

	singular		plural	
	subject	object	subject	object
1st person	I	me	we	us
2nd person	you	you	you	you
3rd person	he/she/it	him/her/it	they	them

Possessives

Possessives can stand alone:

*Is this book **yours**?*

or they can be used with nouns:

*Is this **your** book?*

	singular		plural	
	with nouns	stand alone	with nouns	stand alone
1st person	my	mine	our	ours
2nd person	your	yours	your	yours
3rd person	his/her/its	his/hers/its	their	theirs

Reflexive pronouns
myself, yourself, himself, herself, itself, ourselves, yourselves, themselves

Demonstrative pronouns
this, that, these, those

Indefinite pronouns
someone, somebody, something, anyone, anybody, anything

Relative pronouns
who, whom, which, that

Interrogative pronouns
who, whom, which, what

Word classes

Pronoun guidelines

The most important thing about pronouns is to make sure that people know clearly who or what you are talking about. Look at this short paragraph:

> Peter was having an argument with Clare and Rachel. **She** (1) is a vegetarian but **they** (2) couldn't agree what being a vegetarian means. Peter thought you could eat eggs and fish, but Clare said you couldn't … Rachel said **she** (3) was confused about the difference between vegetarians and vegans. Peter said **they** (4) were mad – he liked a nice steak, himself.

None of the pronouns in **bold** type is clear:

1 'She' could mean Clare or Rachel.
2 'They' could mean all three of them, or any two of them.
3 'She' could mean either Clare or Rachel herself.
4 'They' could mean Clare and Rachel, or vegetarians and vegans.

Always check your writing to make sure that it is clear what each pronoun refers to.

Exercise D

From the following text, write down:
- two personal pronouns
- two possessives
- two relative pronouns.

Tony likes to spend Saturdays curled up with a book or playing his flute, but his parents expect him to play football. 'It's what my dad did and your dad did. It's what boys do and we expect you to do it,' says his mum.

But compare Tony's plight with Wendy's. Wendy's parents expect her to spend Saturdays window-shopping or painting her toenails. 'It's what your mum did when she was a girl. I expect no less from you,' says her dad. But Wendy wants to spend Saturdays playing rugby. She's got the legs and shoulders for it and, to use her own words, she's a born rugger player. But her parents have pointed out that she was born a girl. They took her rugby boots to Oxfam, gave her a shopping bag and a bottle of nail varnish and told her to start painting.

I know at least fifty boys who spend Saturdays with a book or a musical instrument, but I don't know any girls who play rugby on Saturdays or any other day. Which proves that parents are tougher on girls and stick to their expectations, but give in to boys and let them do as they want.

Word classes

Prepositions

What are prepositions?

The easiest way to answer this question is to make a list of the commonest ones:

about	after	as	at	before	behind
between	by	during	for	from	in
into	of	on	over	than	through
to	under	with	within	without	

How do we use prepositions?

Prepositions come before one of the following:

◆ **a noun**
   under <u>water</u>

◆ **an adjective**
   in <u>purple</u>

◆ **a pronoun**
   beside <u>me</u>

◆ **a noun phrase**
   outside <u>my Uncle Arthur's garden</u>

Word classes

Exercise E

Read the following text, and write down two examples of each of these:
- a preposition followed by a pronoun
- a preposition followed by a noun
- a preposition followed by a noun phrase.

In the beginning there weren't any tabloid newspapers to report what was going on in the world. In fact there wasn't a world until an Almighty Male called God created it and all the creatures in it. The last of the creatures He made was a man called Adam, who bore a strong resemblance to the ape. 'He's my first attempt at a human,' thought God. 'I'll have another go.' He couldn't be bothered to start again from scratch so he decided to make the improved version out of Adam's rib.

'Out of my rib!' squawked Adam.

He was so terrified he fell to the ground in a faint (no man has been brave enough to give birth since).

When he came to, however, it was all over and he saw another human standing beside him.

'She's a woman,' said God. 'Her name is Eve.' Eve's body curved gracefully, her face wasn't hairy and she had no knobbles on her knees. 'I have to say, Adam, she's a definite improvement on you,' said God.

God put Adam and Eve in the Garden of Eden, a place of great beauty where the sun always shone, lions and lambs snuggled up together and mosquitoes didn't bite. He told them they could live there in everlasting bliss. 'All I ask in return is that you don't eat that apple.' He pointed to a nearby tree with a large red apple on it.

'Aye, aye, God. Whatever you say,' said Adam.

But Eve was curious. 'Why can't we eat it?'

'Because if you do you'll find out all sorts of things you'd wish you hadn't. All I want is for you to be happy. I'll do everything for you,' said God, 'and give you everything you need. You won't have to worry about a thing.'

Word classes

Conjunctions

Using conjunctions

Conjunctions are used to join things together. We can use them to join:

◆ **words**
*tired **but** happy*

◆ **phrases**
*the headteacher **and** all the staff*

◆ **clauses**
*She saw the letter **when** she got home.*

What are conjunctions?

Here are two lists which include the commonest conjunctions:

A
and	but	nor	or	then	yet

These conjunctions are used to join together things that are equally important:

> *chicken and chips*
> *I'll tell her, or you can tell her.*

There are other conjunctions which join things together in a different way. They give information about **when**, **where** or **why** as well as **other information**:

B

When
after	before	since	until	when	while

Where
after	before	where	wherever

Why
as	because	since	so

Other information
although	if	though	unless

Conjunctions guidelines

There is a lot more about conjunctions on pages 126–30.

Phrases

A phrase is a group of words built up on a single word. Phrases are important 'building blocks' of sentences. The following sentence illustrates the main kinds of phrase:

VERB PHRASE

My little brother Julian has been playing in the garden.

NOUN PHRASE   PREPOSITIONAL PHRASE

Noun phrases

What is a noun phrase?

A noun phrase is a group of words built up on a single noun. This noun is called the **headword**. In these noun phrases the headword is printed in **bold** type:

> the new **captain**
> that **person** over there

Noun phrases can be the subject, object or complement of a sentence:

> **the new captain** is Sandra Nicholls. SUBJECT
> We have just chosen **the new captain**. OBJECT
> Sandra has become **the new captain**. COMPLEMENT

There is more about this on pages 118 and 121–2.

How do noun phrases work?

You start with a noun headword: *bicycle*

Then you gradually add words before it:

> my **bicycle**
> my new **bicycle**
> my brand new **bicycle**

You can also add words after it:

> my brand new **bicycle** with a yellow frame

So a noun phrase can have these parts:

WORDS BEFORE	HEADWORD	WORDS AFTER
my brand new	**bicycle**	with a yellow frame

Phrases

Headword

All noun phrases have a headword, which is a noun.

Words before

Adjectives usually come before the noun – and you can have quite a string of them:

> my **new fast yellow** bicycle

There is another group of words which usually come before adjectives. They are called **determiners**:

DETERMINERS	ADJECTIVES	HEADWORD
the	new English	teacher
her	latest romantic	film

Common determiners are:

◆ *an, the* (these words are called **articles**)

◆ *my, her, your*, etc.

◆ *this, that, these, those*

◆ *some, any, more, less, many, few, all, both*

◆ *one, two, three*, etc.

Words after

We can also provide a lot of information after the headword. In these noun phrases the headword is printed in **bold** type:

> the **day** when I met Jonno …
> the **woman** in the dark green coat …
> the best **player** in yesterday's match …

Noun phrase guidelines

If writers have problems using noun phrases, it is usually because they let them get too long. They just get out of control:

A large heavy angry-looking man with his hands in his pockets and followed by two nasty-looking thugs were was were coming towards me.

Which should it be: *was* or *were*? The noun phrase (*A large … thugs*) is so long that the writer has lost control. If this starts to happen:

1 Try to break the sentence into bits and start again:
   A large heavy angry-looking man was coming towards me. He had his hands in his pockets and was followed by two nasty-looking thugs.

2 Make sure that you can work out which noun is the headword. That will tell you the correct form of the verb:
   *A large heavy angry-looking **man** with his hands in his pockets and followed by two nasty-looking thugs **was** …*

Phrases

Practice

Exercise A

1. In the following extract a number of noun phrases have been missed out. They are listed at the end in the wrong order. Write the number of each space and the letter of the noun phrase that should go in it.

> There are two kinds of eclipse: _1_, or solar eclipse, which happens when the Moon passes in front of the Sun and blocks its light to the Earth; and _2_, or lunar eclipse, which is when the Moon passes into _3_.
>
> In many ancient civilizations a solar eclipse was thought to be _4_. The Moon can block out our view of the Sun completely, plunging the Earth into darkness and leaving visible only the shimmering halo of the Sun's hot gas atmosphere. _5_ lasted for 7 minutes and 8 seconds – the longest for 1238 years. _6_, on the other hand, may last for up to 1 hour and 44 minutes.

> **A** an omen of terrible misfortunes
>
> **B** total lunar eclipses
>
> **C** an eclipse of the Moon
>
> **D** the total solar eclipse of June 1955
>
> **E** the Earth's shadow
>
> **F** an eclipse of the Sun

2. Use each of the following nouns as the headword for a noun phrase. Make each phrase as long as you can.

> computer   food   beach
> person   success

3. Make a table like the one below and write out the parts of each of your phrases in the correct space:

WORDS BEFORE	HEADWORD	WORDS AFTER
my brand new	bicycle	with a yellow frame

Verb phrases

What is a verb phrase?

The full name for the verb in a sentence is the **verb phrase** – even when it is made up of only one word. But verb phrases are often made up of several words. For example:

> Mrs Brown **marked** our homework yesterday.
> She **was marking** all evening.
> She **should have been marking** again today.

How do verb phrases work?

1. **One word**

   If the verb phrase has only one word, it is a main verb:

   *Mrs Brown **marked** ....*

   There is more about main verbs on pages 97–8.

   Tense

   If the verb phrase contains just one word it can be present tense or past tense. For example:

   > Mrs Brown **marks** our homework every week. *(present tense)*
   > Mrs Brown **marked** our homework last night. *(past tense)*

2. **More than one word**

   If we want to give more information about **when** things happened, we add **auxiliary verbs** to the main verb. (There is more about auxiliary verbs on page 98.)

   By using auxiliary verbs with the main verb, we can make all these tenses:

	SIMPLE	CONTINUOUS	PERFECT	PERFECT CONTINUOUS
PAST	marked	was marking	had marked	had been marking
PRESENT	marks	is marking	has marked	has been marking
FUTURE	will mark	will be marking	will have marked	will have been marking

Of course it's one thing to be able to make tenses – and another to be able to use them all correctly!

Phrases

Other ways of showing *when* something happened

We use the tense of the verb to show when something happened and what it was like. But we can give other information about time. Compare these two sentences:

> At the moment I **am writing** a story about a ferret.
> Tomorrow I **am writing** a story about a pet rabbit.

The difference in time is shown by the words *At the moment* and *Tomorrow*. Some common time expressions are:

today	yesterday	tomorrow	in two days' time
last year	next year	soon	later
afterwards	recently	earlier	once

Verb phrase guidelines

1. Using past tenses in stories

It is very important to use the correct tense when telling a story:

- Stories are usually told using past tenses:
  I went / I was going / I had gone / I had been going

- For simple actions, you use the **simple past**:
  *Pete **dashed** across the road.*

- If one thing happens while something else is going on, you use two tenses:
  *The man **was following** (PAST CONTINUOUS) him, so Pete **dashed** (SIMPLE PAST) across the road.*

- If one thing has finished before another starts you use two tenses:
  *When he **had left** (PAST PERFECT) the man a long way behind, Pete **sat** (SIMPLE PAST) down for a rest.*

- Sometimes you may need as many as four tenses:
  *The man **had been following** (PAST PERFECT CONTINUOUS) Pete for a long time, but Pete **had escaped** (PAST PERFECT). Now it **was raining** (PAST CONTINUOUS) so Pete **sheltered** (SIMPLE PAST) under a tree.*

2. Tenses in descriptions

People sometimes get confused about which tense to use when writing a description.

- If the person, place or thing you are describing still exists and hasn't changed, then use present tenses:
  *He **is** a tall man and often **wears** ragged brown trousers.*

- If it has changed – often in a story – then use past tenses:
  *She saw Mr Davies outside the shed. He **was** a tall man and **wore** ragged brown trousers.*

Phrases

Exercise B

In the extract that follows, a number of verbs have been missed out.
The stems of the missing verbs are listed at the end, in the wrong order.
Write the number of each space and the correct form of the verb that
should fill it.

> As it __1__ the Earth, the Moon __2__ slowly on its own axis – an imaginary
> line drawn through its centre – making one complete revolution in just
> over 29 days. This is the same as the time taken by the Moon to make one
> complete journey around the Earth.
>
> The result is that the same side of the Moon is always turned towards
> the Earth. Centuries-old maps of the Moon __3__ us the same features on
> the face of the Moon that we can see today. It was not until the USSR's
> spacecraft *Luna 3* __4__ the back of the Moon in October 1959 that the
> hidden side __5__ for the first time.
>
> These initial photographic missions to the Moon were followed by a
> series of soft landings by automatic probes. *Luna 16*, launched by the
> USSR in 1970, __6__ the first probe to land on the Moon, take samples, and
> then return safely to Earth. But it was the USA's Apollo programme that
> first managed to land people on the Moon.
>
> On 21 July 1969, the first manned landing on the Moon was made when
> Neil Armstrong and Edwin Aldrin __7__ out on to the Sea of Tranquility,
> while Michael Collins orbited above them in *Apollo 11*'s command
> module, *Columbia*.

> step   photograph   be   turn   show   see   orbit

Exercise C

1. Copy out the table below and write these time words and phrases in
   the correct spaces:

> last year   this year   three years ago   next year
> in two days' time in the old days   nowadays   at present

PAST	PRESENT	FUTURE
yesterday	today	tomorrow

2. Add four more time expressions to the table.

3. Choose three of the time expressions and use each one in a sentence.

Phrases

Prepositional phrases

What are prepositional phrases?

They are groups of words starting with a preposition. As a reminder, these are the commonest prepositions:

about	after	as	at	before	behind
between	by	during	for	from	in
into	of	on	over	than	through
to	under	with	within	without	

These are examples of prepositional phrases:

before midnight	during *Romeo and Juliet*
in red	between us
after my first week at school	

How do we use them?

There are two main ways of using prepositional phrases:

1. **As adverbials**

   Adverbials are words or phrases that form part of a sentence. They mostly answer these questions:

   - **Where?**
     *We left our bikes **behind the bus shelter**.*

   - **When?**
     ***After about ten minutes** a bus arrived.*

   - **How?**
     *She wrote the letter **in her best handwriting**.*

   Other adverbials **link** two sentences together:
   *Josie forgot to lock her bike. **As a result** it was stolen.*

   Some make **comments** on what has gone before:
   *Josie's bike was stolen. **Between you and me**, I think she was very upset.*

2. **In noun phrases**

   Prepositional phrases can also be part of a noun phrase. For example:
   *the man **in the moon***

   *the woman **in the corner** **of a room** **on the top floor***

   Each of these is a prepositional phrase.

Phrases

Prepositional phrase guidelines

It is very tempting to make a string of prepositional phrases – especially when you want to be very clear about where or when something happened:

> **In a small burrow just by the hedge at the corner of a field in Mr Jones's farm** lived a rabbit.

These can be irritating for the reader. It is sometimes better to break sentences like that into two:

> **In a small burrow just by the hedge** lived a rabbit. The hedge was **at the corner of a field in Mr Jones's farm.**

Exercise D

1. Use each of the following prepositions as the headword of a prepositional phrase:

   > between   without   during   about   under

2. Choose two of the phrases you have made and write a sentence containing each one.

Exercise E

In the extract that follows, a number of prepositional phrases have been missed out. All that has been left is the preposition that starts each one. Write out a suitable prepositional phrase for each space.

> You can be the judge. Am I the biggest liar in _1_ or do I tell the truth? There is one thing for sure – Dad believes me. Anyway, I will leave it up to _2_. I will tell you what happened and you can make up _3_.
>
> It all starts one evening about _4_. Dad is cooking the tea and Mum is watching *Sixty Minutes* on _5_. Suddenly there is a knock on _6_. 'I'll get it,' yells my little brother Matthew. He always runs to be first to the door and first to _7_. It really gets on my nerves the way he does this.
>
> We hear the sound of Matthew talking to an adult. Then we hear heavy footsteps coming down _8_. Everyone looks up and stares at this man wearing a light-blue uniform.

Phrases

Phrases

Adjective and adverb phrases

What are they and how are they used?

An adjective phrase is a group of words built up on an adjective. Usually a word is put in front of the adjective to change its meaning in some way:

> **extremely** *sorry*

The word *extremely* is an adverb and we say that it **modifies** the adjective *sorry*. You can have words after the adjective as well as before it in an adjective phrase:

> *sorry* **for that mistake**

You can make **adverb phrases** in the same way:

> **rather** *quickly*
> *quickly* **for someone her age**

Adjective and adverb phrases guidelines

There is a small number of adverbs that are commonly used in adjective and adverb phrases:

> very   really   extremely   incredibly   ever so

It is easy to over-use these words:

> *The game was ever so exciting. Kerry played really well and Steve was very good. The referee was really terrible and Kerry got very cross …*

What you should remember is that often you can avoid using *very* and *really* by thinking more carefully about the adjectives or adverbs you want to use. Compare these two lists:

quite fast	quick
very fast	fast
really fast	rapid
incredibly fast	high-speed
fantastically fast	express
	hurtling
	jet-propelled
	supersonic

Choosing exactly the right word can save you repeating yourself and stop your readers getting bored.

Parts of a sentence

Different kinds of sentence

There are four different kinds of sentence:

1. Statement
She loves ice cream.

2. Question
Does she love ice cream? (**yes/no question**)
Does she love ice cream or peanut butter sandwiches? (**either/or question**)
What does she love? (**question-word question**)

3. Directive
Give me that ice cream!

4. Exclamation
How she loves ice cream!

Using directives

Directives aren't just about giving orders. We also use them to:

◆ request   ◆ invite

◆ advise   ◆ warn.

◆ instruct

When you are writing instructions or giving advice, you will need to use directive sentences. Try to avoid making your writing sound as if you are standing in the middle of a large square shouting orders at your readers!

Sentences can have these parts:

◆ subject

◆ verb

◆ object

◆ complement

◆ adverbial.

In this chapter the descriptions and explanations are based on statement sentences. These are the commonest kind of sentence. The descriptions and explanations are also based on simple sentences. These are sentences that only contain one verb.

Parts of a sentence

The subject

All complete statement sentences have a subject. The subject usually:

◆ comes at the beginning of a sentence, or near the beginning

◆ comes before the verb

◆ gives us some information about what the sentence is about

◆ is a noun, pronoun or noun phrase.

The subjects of these sentences are printed in **bold** type:

> **She** likes ice cream.
> In the summer **Mary** eats ice cream every day.
> **Chocolate chip and mint ice cream** is her favourite.

Subject guidelines

Remember that the subject often tells us what the sentence is about.

1. If you use a pronoun make sure that it is clear who or what it refers to.

2. If the subject is a noun phrase, don't make it too long. Otherwise your readers may get lost or confused.

Exercise A

Write down the subject in each of the following sentences.

1. They left early.

2. Cars fascinate her.

3. Our English teacher drives a Porsche.

4. Uncle Jamie was the last person to arrive.

5. The last person to arrive was Uncle Jamie.

6. It is unwise to walk around barefoot in the snow.

7. Walking around barefoot in the snow is unwise.

8. *Four Weddings and a Funeral* used to be her favourite film.

9. Much of what we have learned in maths this year is really difficult.

10. Maths isn't my favourite subject.

The verb

All complete statement sentences have a verb. The verb usually:

◆ comes after the subject

◆ comes before the object or complement

◆ describes an action or a state or links the subject to the complement.

The verb can be one word or a group of words. If it is a group of words, all these words are verbs.

In these sentences, the verbs are all printed in **bold** type:

All the best CDs **have gone**.
Maria does not **want to do** her maths homework.
Peter Dart **was** first in the 200 metres.
Yesterday the police **closed** the High Street.

Verb guidelines

1. Finite verb

A complete sentence must contain a finite verb. This table shows which parts of the verb are finite and which are not:

STEM	walk	go	do	have	be
INFINITIVE	to walk	to go	to do	to have	to be
PRESENT PARTICIPLE	walking	going	doing	having	being
PAST PARTICIPLE	walked	gone	done	had	been
PRESENT TENSE	walk/walks	go/goes	do/does	has/have	is/am/are
PAST TENSE	walked	went	did	had	was/were

These are the finite forms.

If there is more than one word in the verb phrase, then the first word should be a finite verb.

2. Agreement

The verb must **agree** with the subject:

It is particularly important to check the agreement of the verb if the subject is a long noun phrase.

I **am** very happy about Mary's visit.
Mary **is** coming here tomorrow.
We **are** having a party

Parts of a sentence

Exercise B

In the text that follows, some of the sentences are numbered and printed in **bold type**. Write down the number of each sentence and then its verb. Make sure that you write down the whole of the verb.

The fenland was as flat as the sea. (1) The woman walking on the low bank turned to look behind her. A line of distant trees was like the shadow under the lip of a wave about to roll in from the horizon. **There was nothing to stop it.** (2) The heat of the day was intense but she shuddered.

There was a man with her, a little way ahead. (3) He raised his arms and drank in the air. **'Marvellous!' he said.** (4)

She turned to look in the other direction. (5) The flat land reached away into the sea itself, turning first into sleek mud before, far away, the glazed sea lay over it.

'Marvellous!' said the man again.

The grass was coarse where they walked, but beyond the bank it lay in lush green clots smoothed and limp where the tide had left them. **And then the mud gently humped like the backs of seals.** (6) Except in one place. **Something jutted, rounded but ungainly.** (7)

'What's that?' she said.

He looked where she pointed. 'Don't know,' he said. 'Stump or something.'

'Tom!' **It was almost a cry.** (8) It made his head jerk round towards her. **'It's a body!'** (9)

Statement sentences usually have a subject and a verb. There are three other parts which sentences can contain: object, complement and adverbial.

The object

The object in a statement sentence usually comes after the verb and refers to a different person or thing from the subject.

The object of a sentence can be a noun, a pronoun, or a noun phrase.

In these sentences the objects are printed in **bold** type.

> In the 200 metres David beat **me**.
> Of all the people in our class, I like **Dan**.
> Donna ate **my ice cream**.

Some sentences have two objects:

> The postman brought   my sister Jane   a large parcel.
>   INDIRECT OBJECT   DIRECT OBJECT

Sentences like this can be turned round in this way:

> The postman brought   my sister Jane   a large parcel.
>
> The postman brought   a large parcel   for my sister Jane.

Object guidelines

When the object of a sentence is a personal pronoun, it sometimes has to change its form:

SUBJECT	OBJECT
I	me
we	us
you	you
he/she/it	him/her/it
they	them

The complement

The complement in a statement sentence usually comes after the verb and refers to the same person or thing as the subject.

It is called the **comple**ment because it **comple**tes the subject.

The complement of a sentence can be a noun, a pronoun, a noun phrase, an adjective or an adjective phrase.

Parts of a sentence

In these sentences the complements are printed in **bold** type.

> She seems **happy.**
> It was **you.**
> This is **John.**
> He is **my very best friend.**

The verb in this type of sentence is called a **linking verb** because it links the subject and the complement. By far the commonest linking verb is 'to be' (*am, is, are, was, were,* etc.) Other linking verbs are *'seem', 'appear'* and *'become'.*

Exercise C

In the following text some of the sentences are numbered. In these sentences one part has been printed in **bold type**. Write the number of each sentence and say if the part printed in bold is:

◆ the subject

◆ the direct object

◆ the indirect object

◆ the complement.

He laughed and held her hand. 'It's not **big enough**.' **(1)**

'But it is! Can't you see?'

'No, no, no.' He comforted her, but she would not be convinced. 'All right, I'll prove it,' he said, and he began to take off **his shoes**. **(2)**

'You can't go out there, Tom. **It**'s dangerous. **(3)** Please don't.'

But he was barefoot, slithering down the bank. **The brown mud** squeezed up between his toes and engulfed his white feet. **(4)** 'It's deep,' he said, and bent to roll up his trouser legs.

The woman on the bank bit the knuckles of one clenched fist but said nothing. **(5)** …

He stood up and began to walk. The mud was cold and hugged his feet, reluctant to let him move. It got deeper and he wanted to turn back, but pride made him go on.

The stump was **almost black**. **(6)** It lay at an angle, only partly above the mud, and dark weed clung to it like sparse hair. Like hair. But it was still too small for a body …

The mud was up to his knees and he was moving unsteadily. **The last few yards** were going to be difficult. **(7)**

'Don't touch it!' **Her voice** from behind him was as thin as the wind through grass. **(8)**

The adverbial

Adverbials can come almost anywhere in a sentence. They are much more varied than the other parts of a sentence. These guidelines should help you to spot them.

◆ Many adverbials provide information in answer to the questions:
where? (*downstairs, at the corner of the street*)
when? (*yesterday, in two years' time*)
how? (*slowly, with a flick of her wrist*)

◆ Other adverbials make a link between two sentences:
Samantha lost her purse. **As a result** *she couldn't buy me a birthday present.*

◆ Some adverbials make a comment on an earlier sentence:
Samantha lost her purse. **Fortunately for her** *it was handed in to the police station.*

Very often an adverbial is one of these:

◆ an adverb or adverbial phrase

◆ a prepositional phrase.

In these sentences the adverbials have been printed in **bold** type:

We met **on Saundersfoot beach.**
They got home **after dark.**
She was speaking **in a very loud voice.**

Adverbial guidelines

1. When you are writing a story or report, use **adverbials of time** with care, to make it clear **when** things happened:
I met her **three days ago.** **Before that** *I hadn't seen her* **for over a year**.

2. When you are writing a description, you may need to use adverbials of place:
There is a small stream **at the bottom of the hill**. *A tall silver birch grows* **beside it**, *shading the grassy bank.*

3. Some adverbials can come in more than one place in the sentence. Make sure that you put them in the right place.

Parts of a sentence

Exercise D

A number of adverbials have been missed out from the passage that follows. They are listed at the end in the wrong order. Write the number of each blank and the adverbial that should go in it. After each adverbial write down what type it is:

a adverbial answering the question **where?**

b adverbial answering the question **when?**

c adverbial answering the question **how?**

 _1_ he waved to reassure her.

 _2_ his raised hand was clenched as though he was fighting to keep his balance. She could not see his face. The corners of his mouth were pulled back _3_ , his eyes stared, white-rimmed. For the stump was moving, turning _4_ to point at him. Slowly, slowly, and his feet were trapped.

'Aaaaaaah!' The sound in his throat was too small to reach her but she could see the stump. The blunt end of it seemed _5_ to seek him and then suddenly it went blind. A slight quiver and it laid itself _6_ down. He looked at it, panting. A waterlogged stump. Since the last tide it had been _7_ . He had disturbed the mud and laid it to rest.

'Come back!' She was pleading.

His skin had gone cold. _8_ he was sweating. He laughed at himself and hauled one of his feet clear to turn towards her.

'Only a bit of wood,' he called. 'Told you!'

As he climbed the bank he said, 'A piece of bog oak isn't a body.'

But she was pale. 'Let's go back,' she said. I don't care what it is, it's evil.'

He laughed as he tore handfuls of grass to clean the mud from his feet. 'Your imagination!' he said. 'It even gets me going at times.'

gently	on the point of overbalancing
without turning round	suddenly
for another second	like a black finger
now	in a snarl

Multiple sentences

All the sentences that have been used in the examples so far in this section have been simple sentences. A **simple sentence** is one that contains one subject and one finite verb:

SUBJECT	VERB	REST OF SENTENCE
Peter	likes	apples.
My brother Dave's best friend at his last school	used to enjoy eating	those large sour green apples called Bramleys.

As you can see, simple sentences are not always short. They can be quite long. The word 'simple' tells us about the grammar, not the number of words!

Exercise A

The extract that follows contains six simple sentences and three 'sentences' that do not contain finite verbs. Which are they?

> Hi. I'm Luce. Unfortunately.
>
> When you're stuck with a name like Luce, believe me you come in for one big crateful of abuse. Hey! That rhymes, doesn't it? Maybe I'm following in Mum's footsteps. She's always writing poetry. She's obsessed with it. Oops, I've gone off the point already. I'm sorry, I can't help it. It's because I'm the crazy one, I suppose. I can't say I'm any more over the moon with my image than I am with my name, but unfortunately I'm stuck with them both. I'll tell you why.

Clauses

A unit that contains a subject and a verb is called a **clause**. A clause that can stand on its own, like *Peter likes apples,* is a simple sentence. A sentence that contains more than one clause is called a **multiple sentence**. The following multiple sentence contains three clauses:

Mary likes oranges, but Peter likes apples and Deirdre hates all fruit.
    CLAUSE   +   CLAUSE   +   CLAUSE

Multiple sentences

Compound sentences

The simplest way of joining clauses is to stick them together using these words, called **conjunctions**:

and	but	then	or	nor	yet

Sentences that are made by joining clauses using these conjunctions are called **compound sentences**. As you can see, each of them gives the sentence a different meaning. Compare these sentences:

> It poured with rain **and** the team lost.
> It poured with rain **but** the team lost
> It poured with rain **then** the team lost.

Exercise B

Make up compound sentences using each of the six conjunctions in the list.

Complex sentences

Conjunctions like *and* and *but* can only tell us a little about how the clauses in the sentence are linked. If we want to say more complicated things, we have to use a different kind of sentence and a different kind of conjunction:

> **Because** it poured with rain the team lost.
> **After** it poured with rain the team lost.
> **Before** it poured with rain the team lost.
> **Although** it poured with rain the team lost.

In sentences like these, one of the clauses is the **main** clause. The other **subordinate** clauses depend on this clause to make sense:

SUBORDINATE CLAUSE	MAIN CLAUSE
Because it poured with rain	the team lost.
After it poured with rain	the team lost.

It isn't always easy to work out which is the main clause and which are the subordinate clauses. The thing to remember is that the main clause is the only one that can stand on its own. In the example, you can take the clause *the team lost* and it makes a sentence on its own. You can't do this to *Because it poured with rain*.

Multiple sentences

Exercise C

Make up four complex sentences. For each one use two clauses from the left-hand column and a different conjunction from the right-hand column:

CLAUSES	CONJUNCTIONS
school was closed	because
we went to Seaford	before
Dee and Marie were on holiday	after
we met Sam	although
we stayed at home	

Exercise D

Write down the main clause from each of these sentences:

1. It started raining after we reached home.

2. Before I go to bed, I must finish my English homework.

3. Although there's a TV programme I want to see, I've promised to ring Helen.

4. Mrs Grayson was angry because I left all my books at home.

When, where, why, etc.

The best way to understand more about how complex sentences work is to look at the different ways they can help you when you write.

We can use complex sentences to give information about:

◆ the **time when** things happened
◆ the **place** where they happened
◆ the **reason** why they happened
◆ **what** the **result** was
◆ **what** the **purpose** was.

We can also combine clauses using words like *if, unless* and *although*.

Time

The commonest conjunctions for talking about time are:

when	while	before	after	since	as	until

It happened **when** I was in Bognor.
I must have done it **since** I got home.
You can't go out **until** you've finished your homework.

Multiple sentences

Exercise E

A detective has been watching a suspect. She has kept a diary of what she has observed:

Later the detective has to write a report. Use her notes to write five sentences. Each of them must contain one of the time conjunctions in the list on page 127.

0921	Suspect leaves house. Walks along Broad Street towards town centre.
0934	Suspect reaches Marks + Spencer, goes in. Wanders round aimlessly. Goes to Food Hall, buys apples and oranges.
1003	Leaves M+S, walks along High St.
1007	Sits on bench opposite Lloyds Bank.
1014	Gets up and goes to newsagent. Buys copy of Daily Express.
1018	Returns to bench. Reads paper. Smokes cigarette.

Place

The commonest conjunctions for talking about place are:

> where   wherever

> They met **where** they usually meet.
> You could bump into them **wherever** there's a chip shop.

Explaining things: reasons, results and purposes

When you write you often need to explain that something happened **because** something else happened, or **as a result of** something else happening.

The commonest conjunctions for talking about reason are:

> because   since   as

> She's come home soaking wet **because** she went out without a coat.
> **Since** it's the holidays, you can stay out later.
> **As** it's mine, I want it back.

The commonest conjunctions for talking about result and purpose are:

> so   so that

> The team put in extra practice **so that** they would win the next game.
> Half of them went down with 'flu, **so** they lost heavily.

Multiple sentences

Exercise F

Make up four complex sentences. For each one use two clauses from the left-hand column and a different conjunction from the right-hand column. You can change 'Damon Hardacre' to 'him' as you need to.

CLAUSES	CONJUNCTIONS
Damon Hardacre is a bully	because
no one likes Damon Hardacre	since
Damon Hardacre has spots	as
people avoid Damon Hardacre	so
Damon Hardacre is very unhappy	so that
I feel sorry for Damon Hardacre	

If

Sometimes you want to write about things that haven't happened, but which could happen.

If you're going out, take your raincoat.

Why?

If it rains, you'll get wet.

If it rained, I'd come home.

Multiple sentences

What makes **if** sentences more complicated is that we can make up different versions of the same sentence:

> **a** If Andy lends me £5 I will be able to buy that new CD.
> **b** If Andy lent me £5 I would be able to buy that new CD.

Both these sentences are about something that has not yet happened – it is still in the future. In sentence (**a**) the person speaking has an open mind about it all: Andy may lend the money or he may not. We don't know. In sentence (**b**) the speaker thinks that it is not very likely that Andy will lend the money.

We can also write **if** sentences about the past:

> **c** If Andy had lent me the money I would have bought that new CD.

Now we *know* that Andy didn't lend the money, but the speaker is still thinking about that new CD!

There is another kind of **if** sentence, and one which you often hear people say:

> **d** If I were Andy, I'd give her the money.

This is impossible. The speaker can *never* be Andy! It's just a way of speaking.

So there are four main kinds of **if** sentence:

a about the future, keeping an open mind

b about the future, talking about things that are rather unlikely to happen

c about the past, talking about things that didn't happen, but thinking about what *might* have happened

d ones that could never happen – impossible ones.

There is one more kind of **if** sentence that is different – and which you may have come across in science lessons:

> **d** If you lower the temperature of water to 0° Celsius, it freezes.

This kind of sentence isn't about the past or the future. It tells us about things that always happen.

Punctuation

Sentences

Everyone knows that you start a sentence with a capital letter and end it with a full stop. But missing out capital letters and full stops is one of the commonest mistakes people make when they write. Most people do it from time to time. If you can understand *why* you do this and *how* to avoid it, your writing will become much easier to read.

Why?

There are only two reasons why people make this mistake:

1. They stop a sentence before it is complete. So instead of writing a full sentence, they write an incomplete one and put a full stop after it:

   Having got to the bus stop just round the corner from Jan's house.

   This 'sentence' is incomplete because it is missing:

   • a subject

   • a finite (complete) verb.

   You could make it into a complete sentence by giving it a subject and making the verb into a finite verb:

   *I **had got** to the bus stop just round the corner from Jan's house.*
   SUBJECT   FINITE VERB

   Or you could add more words to the end of the sentence and give it a subject and a finite verb like this:

   Having got to the bus stop just round the corner from Jan's house,
   ***Peter waited** for the bus.*
   SUBJECT   FINITE VERB

2. The other reason is even commoner. People don't stop when they get to the end of the sentence but go straight on into the next one:
   Peter caught the next bus that came along he went as far as Plowston at the end of the High Street he got off.

   Here three sentences have been rolled into one:
   Peter caught the next bus that came along.
   He went as far as Plowston.
   At the end of the High Street he got off.

   It's easy enough to correct this mistake, if you realize you are making it, *but this takes practice.*

Punctuation

How?

There are two ways in which you can check whether you are dividing your writing into correct sentences:

1. **Read aloud what you have written.** You should find that there are natural breaks in the writing every so often. These are usually where full stops should come (or where you need another 'big' punctuation mark like a colon or semi-colon – see page 134).

2. **Check the grammar** – especially if you are not sure whether you have written a full sentence or not. Ask yourself:

   • What is the subject?

   • What is the finite verb?

Every statement sentence normally has a subject and a finite verb. If you can't find them, then the chances are that what you have written is incomplete.

Exercise A

1. The text that follows has not been correctly divided into sentences. Rewrite it adding full stops and capital letters where necessary:

> Ben knew exactly where his enemy would be waiting and there was nothing he could do about it school was only a minute's walk from the front door but you had to pass the churchyard and that's where Barry would be he always was you could set off early – quarter past eight even – and he'd be there or you could wait till seconds before the bell then run and he'd come loping out throwing his arms round you from behind and trailing his feet till his weight stopped you they got up early at Cansfield Farm and Barry didn't mind waiting he didn't mind being late either so you couldn't win.

2. This is part of a transcript: a piece of spoken English written down as it was spoken. Turn it into written sentences by adding punctuation:

> Father was deafened by the guns at Passchendaele he went to Canada but had to come back here he was unable to conduct business he was always very keen on horses and game birds and things and he used to amuse himself with that and he rented some fields down the road and he used to operate from that we had this little field behind the house old English game was his favourite he was very famous and he hunted and he used to bring on young horses and that sort of thing and he was a very good judge of a horse he used to show a lot of horses anything connected with horses he was very interested in I always had a horse about me and dogs he was very keen on dogs too.

Commas

When a sentence is more than about ten words long, you may need to use commas to divide it into shorter, more manageable sections. These are some of the occasions when you should think of using commas:

1. **To separate the items in a list:**
   She had such a lot of things to do: finish her French homework, feed the dog, phone Carol, and write a shopping list.

   Some people say that you don't need a comma before the 'and' in a list, but it can be useful:
   There are some things I just can't stand: mustard, soggy chips, bacon, and tomatoes.

   If you miss out the comma, it isn't clear whether it is bacon and tomatoes together that the writer doesn't like, or the two things separately.

2. **Before and/or after a subordinate clause:**
   If you don't stop doing that, I shall scream.
   They were all alone, because the rest of the audience had left.

   Subordinate clauses usually begin with a conjunction like *because*, *if*, *unless*, *as* or *when*. There is more about conjunctions on pages 126–30 and more about subordinate clauses on pages 125–6.

   You don't always have to use a comma in sentences like these, but you should think about it.

3. **To put a word or words 'in brackets':**
   The last headteacher, a certain Mrs Staines, retired to Chichester.

   In these sentences, the words between the 'brackets' could be missed out and the sentence would still make sense.

You should always use a comma if it helps avoid confusion. This sentence, for example, needs a comma:

As the soldier attacked the audience in the cinema held their breath.

Other uses
Commas are also sometimes used:

◆ **in addresses on letters and envelopes:**

Many people miss these commas out.

◆ **in direct speech**

This is explained on page 137.

2, The Esplanade,
Boreham-by-Sea,
Wessex,
RT14 8GB

Punctuation

Exercise B

All the commas in this extract have been missed out. Work out where they should go:

> It was not very long after this that there occurred the first of the mysterious events that rid us at last of the captain though not as you will see of his affairs. It was a bitter cold winter with long hard frosts and heavy gales; and it was plain from the first that my poor father was little likely to see the spring. He sank daily and my mother and I had all the inn upon our hands; and were kept busy enough without paying much regard to our unpleasant guest.
>
> It was one January morning very early – a pinching frosty morning – the cove all grey with hoar-frost the ripple lapping softly on the stones the sun still low and only touching the hilltops and shining far to seaward. The captain had risen earlier than usual and set out down the beach his cutlass swinging under the broad skirts of the old blue coat his brass telescope under his arm his hat tilted back upon his head.

Colons

Colons are used:

1. **to introduce a list**
   She had such a lot of things to do: finish her French homework, feed the dog, phone Carol and write a shopping list.

2. **To introduce something else, such as a piece of speech:**
   This is what she said to us: 'If you all work hard and are very lucky you may one day be rich.'

3. **To divide two parts of a sentence that are equal, or balanced:**
   Some people are born lucky: other people have to make their own luck.

Semi-colons

Semi-colons have two main uses:

1. Sometimes you have two sentences that could be separated using a full stop, but which are very closely linked together by their meaning. You can show this link by using a semi-colon **instead of a full stop**.
   Sometimes I just know that we're going to win; today's match wasn't one of them.

2. You can also use semi-colons **instead of commas** to separate the items in a list, when each item is quite long:
   I had had enough: Mary had failed to turn up; I had lost all my money; there was thick fog everywhere; and all the buses had stopped running.

Exercise C

Most of the punctuation has been removed from this extract. Write it out adding all the necessary punctuation marks:

> he wondered if he would ever speak to her again on past experience probably not shyness he thought not for the first time should be treated as an illness for years people had been telling him he'd grow out of it now more than sixteen he still hadn't in fact he suffered worse than ever another wasted opportunity he told himself with familiar self-punishing anger like the one last week in the High Street with Sue Pritchard and the one before that in the drama studio with Ellen Mitchell who everyone said was a doddle to chat up and the one before that with Jane Carpenter in the underpass when there wasn't even anyone else around to put him off and the one before that and that and that he slammed the back door behind him and instantly blushing as usual regretted it if she were still there she'd hear think him a blunderer and laugh

Apostrophes

Apostrophes are used:

1. to show that **letters have been missed out**:

   | he had | — | he'd |
   | will not | — | won't |

2. to show that something belongs to someone (**possession**):

   John's book
   My parents' car.

It is the second use that causes problems. The easiest way to get it right is to ask yourself, 'What letter does the word end with?' If it ends with any letter except an 's', you add an apostrophe followed by an 's'. If it ends with an 's', then just add the apostrophe.

Remember:

| it's = it is | who's = who is |
| its = of it | whose = of whom |

Punctuation

Script

A **script** is a way of writing down a conversation. It is used in plays and to write down recorded conversations. The main purpose of a script is to write down all the words spoken by each person. It is usually set out like this:

SANDY: Are you sure the repair-man can't make it, Mum?
MOTHER: I'm sorry, Sandy, but the video set's broken down and that's that.
         The repair-man can't come to fix it till tomorrow.
SANDY: Aw, Mum! This is so boring! Stuck inside on a wet Saturday afternoon
         with nothing to do – no video to watch and only party political
         broadcasts on the telly! I'll die of boredom!

Rules

1. Write characters' names in capital letters.

2. Put a colon after the character's name.

3. Indent the speech. Write exactly what each character says and do *not* use inverted commas.

Other information

A script can contain extra information:

1. a description of the setting:

Scene 1
Sandy's house. Enter SANDY and her MOTHER. MOTHER is carrying a book.
SANDY: Are you sure the repair-man can't make it, Mum?

2. a description of what each character does (sometimes called **stage directions**):

SANDY: You know I hate reading, Mum!
MOTHER: (*waving the book in front of her*) Oh, go on, try this book that your
         Auntie Angela bought you for your birthday.

3. a description of how a character says a particular sentence or speech:

SANDY: (*grudgingly*) Oh, all right.

In printed books (and in word-processed scripts) this information is usually printed in *italics*. In handwriting you can underline the words. In each case put the information in brackets. All this helps the actors to see what are instructions and what are words they say.

Punctuation

Direct speech

Direct speech is also a way of writing down exactly the words people say. It is used in stories and reports:

> 'This is Rick,' said Vonnie. 'Ricky Brooke. And I need some money.'
> 'Keep your fingers out of that till!'
> They were in her mother's dress shop, and Vonnie Lawson was leaning against the cash register. 'I need money, Mother, please! It's vital!'
> 'It always is. So what's so important this time?'
> 'You won't like it if I tell you.'

Main rules

1. The actual words spoken are always placed between inverted commas. You can use single: ' ', or double: " ". Make sure that you always use the same ones.

2. At the end of each section of speech, there must be a comma, a full stop, a question mark or an exclamation mark **before** the closing inverted commas:
   'Keep your fingers out of that till**!**'

3. Each time there is a new speaker, start a new paragraph and indent it.

4. If you use words like 'she said' before the speech, put a comma or a colon before the opening inverted commas:
   She said, 'Keep your fingers out of that till!'

5. If you use words like 'she said' after the speech, end the speech with a comma before the inverted commas:
   'This is Rick,' said Vonnie.

Exercise D

1. Write the script on page 136 as direct speech.

2. Write the conversation at the top of this page as a script.

3. The words that follow on the next page are part of a conversation. You are not told who is speaking or what is going on.

   • Read it through and work out what is going on.

   • Work out who says each line.

   • Write it out as a full script with a description of the settings and other stage directions.

Punctuation

– Stand still!

– Are they gone, Nosher?

– Quiet, Sid! (*Pause*) Yeah! Heh, heh! I think we've shaken them off at last!

– What do we do now, Nosher?

– We've got to get as far away from those police and prison guards as possible if we want to make good our escape.

– One of them nearly got us, Nosher – I wonder what happened to him?

– He was – shall we say – unavoidably detained.

– Oh! I see ... I think. What now, Nosher?

– We've got to find food, my little friend, so we'll have to find some people who will very kindly give us some.

– D'you think they will, Nosher?

– I think they will, Sid.

– How do you know, Nosher?

– 'Cos I'll be asking them with this! Courtesy of our policeman friend, who now sleeps the sleep of the innocent. Come on, Sid – let's go.

Abbreviations

Sometimes it is convenient to shorten a word or phrase – to **abbreviate** it. Abbreviations take these forms:

1. The first letter of each word being abbreviated:
British Broadcasting Corporation ⟶ *BBC*

2. The first and the last letters of the word:
Mister ⟶ *Mr*

3. The first part of a word:
January ⟶ *Jan.*

These are the rules:

1. If the abbreviation contains the first letter of each word, these are usually capital letters. You can put a full stop after each one, but if it is a common abbreviation (like *BBC*), these full stops are often left out.

2. If it is made of the first and last letter of a word, then you use a small letter for the last letter. The first letter can be a capital or a small letter: it depends on the word. *Mr* begins with a capital, because it is a person's title. There is no need for full stops.

3. If the abbreviation is the first part of a word, write this part in the usual way and end it with a full stop.

Punctuation

Other uses for capital letters

Capital letters are used for names and other proper nouns (see page 94):

Julian   Italy   January

We also use capitals for **proper names**. These are phrases that work in the same way as proper nouns. The difference is that not all the words have capital letters. Basically the 'big words' (nouns, verbs, advjectives, adverbs) have capitals and the 'small words' (the rest) do not:

> Language Kit
> The Taming of the Shrew
> The House of Commons

Exercise E

The following three extracts have been printed without any punctuation at all. Write each one out with the correct punctuation:

1.

some inventions are made to solve a problem in 1903 for example albert parkhouse was working in a wire factory making frames for lampshades when he came back from lunch one day he found all the coat pegs had been used up and there was nowhere to put his coat he snatched up a piece of his wire bent it into the shape of a coathanger and twisted a hook on the top hed invented the worlds first wire coathanger and now billions of people use them his boss saw the hanger copied it and started manufacturing wire coathangers the man made a lot of money from this albert parkhouse got nothing

2.

after the first road fatality in britain in 1896 the coroner said this must never happen again but it has nearly twenty-five million times world-wide since then over 1.5 million crashes have happened in the us alone where the first occurred on 13 september 1899 a certain mr h h bliss stepped off his trolley-car after a journey into new york city at that point a mr a smith driving a new electric cab tried to overtake the trolley-car mr bliss stepped into his path and into history as the first automobile fatality in the usa

3.

hey locky come over here a minute

what for ben was suspicious wayne daykin wasnt a friend and neither were the three lads with him it would be a shame to dodge barry and then get done over by somebody else

what dyou mean what for ive got something to tell you bonehead

ben went over to them what

you know cansfield farm

something kicked in bens chest and he said its barry right somethings happened to him

naw daykins eyes mocked dont you wish though locky eh

dont we all said one of the other boys and everybody laughed

Test practice 1

Section C

This section of the paper is a test of writing. You will be assessed on:

◆ *your ideas and the way you organize and express them*

◆ *your ability to write clearly, using paragraphs and accurate grammar, spelling and punctuation.*

Read the texts on pages 142–4. The first two texts are articles from a local newspaper; the third is a page from a reporter's notebook; the fourth is a page from the Website of the RSPCA, dealing with some 'tricky problems'.

*When you have read the texts choose **one** of the following:*

EITHER:

a Imagine you are a staff writer for a magazine which people read for light entertainment.

Write a feature article that brings together some interesting and unusual news stories about animals.

You should use the information in texts 1, 2 and 3. Try to give your article a theme that unites all three stories. For example it might be:

'The dangers faced by animals in today's world'

or
'Animals are survivors'

or
'The British are mad about animals'

or a theme of your own choosing.

OR

b **Write a news report based on the notes in text 3.**

Follow the same style of writing as the other newspaper reports. Give your story a suitable headline.

OR

c Think of how the incidents described in texts 1 and 2 could have been avoided. **Write a question-and-answer page giving advice – following the pattern of the Web page shown in text 4.**

1

Talbot the cat survives 145F in car plant paint shop

Talbot the tabby cat lost one of his nine lives after being carried by a conveyor belt into an oven used to bake the paint on cars. The moggie miraculously survived despite spending 30 minutes at a searing 145F*.

He mistakenly hitched a ride on the car production line at the Peugeot plant in Coventry and was carried into the oven. When he came out the other side, still clinging to the car, he was still alive – but suffering from badly burned paws and shock.

Worried workers hosed him down and called the RSPCA. Inspector Paul Kempson said: 'All four pads on his paws were burnt off and his whiskers and coat were slightly singed. But it is astounding that he survived that sort of temperature for that length of time.' Staff named the tabby cat after a vintage Peugeot. He is now recovering in an RSPCA home.

* 145F = 65°C

Shock as dog runs off with news sign

A radio appeal for a wayward dog was launched – after it ran off with a metal advertising sign attached to its neck. The petulant pooch made a break for it after becoming restless outside SMS News in Scheregate Steps, Colchester.

Its owner had tied the dog up and went shopping but the animal gave up waiting and wandered off on its own – with its leash still firmly tied to a three-foot high *Evening Gazette* sign.

Newsagent owner Sam Sathan said: 'The dog must have been either frightened by something or bored – it had waited for a while. It just ran across the road and got lost in the dark.'

A keen pet lover himself, Mr Sathan contacted SGR and asked the station to alert the owner that their dog had scarpered. 'I made a request asking for the person who had tied up the dog outside my shop to check the area,' he said. 'I was very concerned about the poor animal.'

Shortly afterwards the metal board turned up outside Mr Sathan's newsagents, battered and broken. However there was no sign of the dog or its owner. 'No-one came inside the store to let me know what had happened,' he said. 'Hopefully the dog has now been reunited with its owner.'

Mr Sathan is now looking into the possibility of installing pegs outside his shop so pet owners have somewhere to tie up their dogs.

3

Cat burglar story
Jillian and John (truck driver) live in Cheltenham, Glos.
They have a Siamese cat called 'Saya'.
Local people have been missing their socks recently – disappearing
mysteriously from their houses.
It began in September.
Then Jillian and John found Saya's basket was full of socks.
In the 8 weeks since Christmas it's collected 33 socks.
Some are in pairs and some are odd.
Jillian: 'My main worry is it must be costing someone a lot of
money. She has brought home so many now it is just getting
ridiculous. It must be the smell of the sock that attracts her.'
John: 'It's a pain in the backside. It's so embarrassing.'

4

WebWiz

Back Forward Stop Refresh Home Search Mail Favorites Larger Smaller Preferences

Address:

Channels \ Favorites \ History \ Search

Animal advice

My school fair is giving away a goldfish as a prize.

The RSPCA believes that animal ownership is a big
responsibility that needs to be planned and well thought
out – not a spur of the moment thing. Games offering
animals as prizes don't take this into consideration.

Very often the animals suffer miserably – goldfish can
easily suffer stress and shock as well as oxygen
starvation, and even die from changes in water
temperature. Many goldfish die before their new owners
get them home – or soon after. If you are concerned
about this issue, ask the event organiser not to give
goldfish as prizes. You may also wish to ask your local
authority to adopt a policy of not allowing animals to be
given as prizes at any fundraising activity held on or in
council-owned land or buildings. This can include fêtes,
circuses and car boot sales.

Test practice 2

Section C

This section of the paper is a test of writing. You will be assessed on:

◆ *your ideas and the way you organize and express them*

◆ *your ability to write clearly, using paragraphs and accurate grammar, spelling and punctuation.*

Read the texts on pages 146–9. The first is a map showing routes up Mount Everest; the second is a page from an information book; the third is a page from a book giving climbers' reactions; the fourth is extracts from reports of an expedition in 1996.

*When you have read the texts choose **ONE** of the following:*

EITHER

a Imagine you have been asked to contribute to an information book for 10–12-year-olds. The subject of the book is 'Human achievement'.

   Write an article called 'Climbing the highest mountain in the world'.

   You should use the information in texts 1, 2, 3 and 4.

OR

b Some people would give anything for the chance to stand on top of the highest mountain in the world. Others just cannot understand what all the fuss is about. Indeed, some would even say that people should be banned from climbing Everest: there is a serious pollution problem; climbers can cause danger not just to themselves but to others as well; and then there's the expense …

   What do you think?

   Write an argument in which you set out the different opinions and explain your own point of view and the reasons for it.

   You should use the material in texts 1, 2, 3 and 4.

OR

c Imagine that you are Sandy Hill Pittman. After you get back safely to the United States, you are asked to write an article about the climb. (Remember that the leader of the expedition, Scott Fischer, was killed in the storm.)

   Write an article about your experiences and feelings about the climb.

   You should use the material in texts 1, 2, 3 and 4.

1

सगरमाथा (SAGARMATHA) **MOUNT EVEREST** 珠穆朗玛峰 (Chomolungma)

2

Everest facts and figures

Height:	29,028 feet/8,850 metres
Local names:	In Nepal: Sagarmatha ('goddess of the sky') In Tibet: Chomolungma ('mother goddess of the universe')
First ascent:	1953, Sir Edmund Hillary and Tenzing Norgay via the South Col Route. Neither has ever said who stepped on the summit first.
Named after:	Mt Everest was named for Sir George Everest in 1859, the British surveyor-general of India.
First oxygenless ascent:	1978, Reinhold Messner and Peter Habeler via the South-East Ridge
First solo ascent:	1980, Reinhold Messner, via the North Col to North Face
First ascent by a woman:	1975, Junko Tabei via the South-East Ridge
Oldest person:	Ramon Blanco (Spain) 60 years, 160 days, 10/7/93
Youngest person:	Shambu Tamang (Nepal) 16, 5/5/73

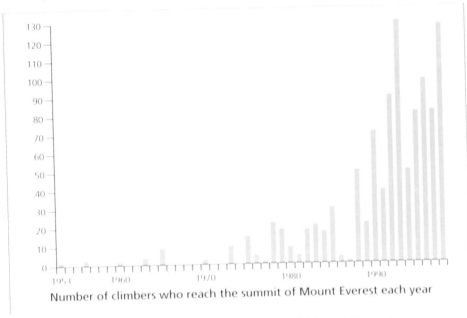

Number of climbers who reach the summit of Mount Everest each year

For every five climbers who reach the summit of Mount Everest, one climber dies on the mountain.

3

What they say ...

What is the use of climbing Mount Everest?
... It is no use. There is not the slightest prospect of any gain whatsoever. ... What we get from this adventure is just sheer joy.
George Leigh Mallory, 1922 – died on the mountain

Well, we knocked the bastard off!
Edmund Hillary, one of first two men to climb Mount Everest

Hey, look, don't worry too much about me.
Rob Hall – died on the mountain: his last words via satellite radio phone to his pregnant wife in New Zealand

Don't forget it's really just a big pile of rocks.
David Breashears

4 What happened in 1996

These extracts are taken from the reports made by Sandy Hill Pittman, an American woman climber, to NBC news. She was a member of the NBC's Everest Assault Expedition:

Wednesday, May 8
Dateline: Camp III, Mt Everest (23,622 ft)

We've made to Camp III, and it's absolutely amazing! … It's dark now, but we have an amazing view down the Western Cwm. It's a 4,000 foot drop from where we sit … I've lost my voice but am doing well.

Tomorrow, we're going to leave around 8 a.m. and reach the South Col by 1 to 3 p.m. Then it's total survival. Leaving our satellite phone at the South Col, we'll set out at midnight from Camp IV and hope to reach the summit at 10 a.m. or noon before the weather turns. If we make it, we'll be the first group up this year.

Thursday, May 9 (2 p.m. ET)
Dateline: South Col, Mt Everest (27,877 ft)

Hi! I'm now at the South Col of Mt Everest. This is probably the highest call I have ever made. We are about to make our summit bid.

At the moment, there are five of us gathered in one tent: Scott and me, Neil, Tim, and Charlotte. As we huddle together we are concentrating on keeping warm, snoozing, and drinking lots of tea and other liquids to keep our bodies well hydrated.

We will get back to you soon. Keep your fingers crossed for some wonderful news from the summit. Talk to you then!

The next day, Sandy Hill Pittman was one of a group of 12 climbers to reach the summit.

Extracts from NBC reports, New York:

Saturday, May 11

On Saturday, five climbers on Mt Everest were reported missing, including NBC's Everest Assault expedition leader Scott Fischer. According to Reuters, four of the missing climbers were part of an expedition led by Rob Hall of New Zealand. Fischer's team summited before several other expeditions, including Rob Hall's. From all indications, when the weather took a turn for the worse and Hall's climbers lagged behind, Fischer went back up toward the summit to help in rescue efforts. …

Sandy Hill Pittman is safe and heading down to Base Camp.

Sunday, May 12

On Sunday, rescue efforts continued as exhausted climbers shuttled up and down the mountain in the aftermath of Friday's severe snowstorm near the summit of Mt Everest. It was difficult to ascertain the status of at least 20 climbers left stranded on the South Col. But there have been at least eight deaths with the body count rising daily.

A total of eight people perished in the storm. In all, during 1996, 98 people reached the summit, and 15 died on the mountain.

Test practice 3

Section C

This section of the paper is a test of writing. You will be assessed on:

◆ *your ideas and the way you organize and express them*

◆ *your ability to write clearly, using paragraphs and accurate grammar, spelling and punctuation.*

Read the texts on pages 151–4. The first is two pages from the Website of the Vegetarian Society; the second is a magazine article; the third is an extract from an interview with a 13-year-old girl.

*When you have read the texts choose **ONE** of the following:*

EITHER

a   Imagine that Claire from text 3 met the writer of text 2. They argue about factory farming and vegetarianism.

Write their argument as a script.

OR

b   There have been a lot of letters in your local paper recently about farming and food. Some are in favour of modern farming and others support the vegetarian point of view.

Write a letter to the paper, expressing your opinion.

You should use the information in texts 1, 2 and 3.

OR

c   Text 1 was written for people of your age. Think about how you might explain to a child of 6 what intensive farming is and what you think about it. (You don't have to agree with the writer of the article.)

Write your explanation and opinion, to be read to a 6-year-old child.

1

WebWiz

Back | Forward | Stop | Refresh | Home | Search | Mail | Favorites | Larger | Smaller | Preferences

Address:

Channels / Favorites / History / Search

Factory farming

Story books show farms as cosy places where hens run around in the yard, pigs wallow in mud and lambs play in the fields. Unfortunately, reality isn't always like that. Most modern farms are more like factories and the animals are treated like food-producing machines. Many animals are kept shut up in crowded sheds their whole life through. Some will have been changed by selective breeding and genetic engineering so that they grow faster, have more offspring, grow more wool or produce more milk than any animal

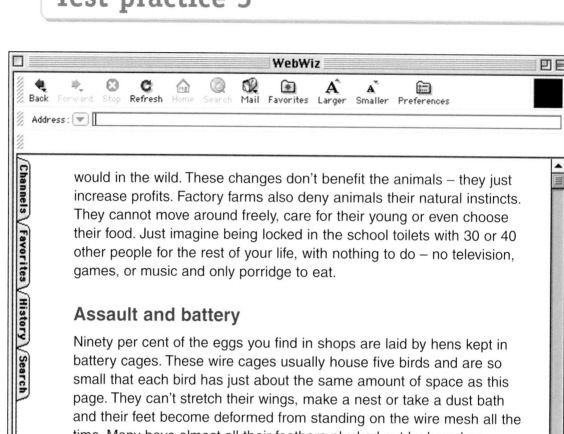

would in the wild. These changes don't benefit the animals – they just increase profits. Factory farms also deny animals their natural instincts. They cannot move around freely, care for their young or even choose their food. Just imagine being locked in the school toilets with 30 or 40 other people for the rest of your life, with nothing to do – no television, games, or music and only porridge to eat.

Assault and battery

Ninety per cent of the eggs you find in shops are laid by hens kept in battery cages. These wire cages usually house five birds and are so small that each bird has just about the same amount of space as this page. They can't stretch their wings, make a nest or take a dust bath and their feet become deformed from standing on the wire mesh all the time. Many have almost all their feathers plucked out by bored or aggressive cage mates. Some birds have their beaks sliced off with a hot wire or blade to stop this feather plucking. Wild hens would live for 12 years, but battery hens are worn out by the time they are two and sent for slaughter.

Killing with kindness?

Lots of people think that it's acceptable to eat meat because they have been told that animals in this country are killed humanely. A pistol with a 15cm bolt is shot into the brain to stun the animal so that it feels no pain when its throat is being cut. But the bolt has to hit the right spot exactly. If the animal moves its head as the pistol is fired, it could end up painfully wounded but fully conscious. One RSPCA report showed that up to half of all young bulls may suffer terrible pain as the stun gun fails to hit the target. Smaller animals are stunned with electric shocks, and poultry are dunked head first into an electrically charged water bath. Many birds don't hang meekly on the conveyor belt, but move around trying to escape. Some move at the wrong time, missing both the stunning bath and the knife. They end up being plunged alive into a scalding tank designed to loosen their feathers after death.

2

A meat-eater's Christmas

Are you brave enough to tackle a goose? They are splendid things and, joy of joys, take unkindly to intensive farming. Geese are as fussy as a great aunt and insist on warmth, good food and more tender loving care than most other farm birds. I once roasted one for an elaborate family banquet. … The goose was enormous. No matter how I tried, the monstrous thing wouldn't go in the oven, and I ended up cutting it in half like a pantomime horse.

Goose can be a fine choice for the big day. It has as much majesty as a turkey, and tastier, juicier meat. Soak up its copious fat with a spice-laden fruit stuffing, or even better, a stuffing of crushed parboiled potatoes, garlic and thyme. I know this sounds a fiddle, but the potato will soak up much of the cooking juices, so we get crisp skin, juicy meat and crumbling, flavour-sodden spuds. Who could ask for more? (Vegetarians can just stay out of this one.)

There is also the tiniest bird of all quail. Sadly, all are farmed now, rather than culled on the heather-covered moors, but what a delectable tangle of bones and flesh these tiny birds are. I have eaten them at Christmas before you can be as greedy as you like but I suggest you allow two or more per person (at least there will be no arguments about who is to do the carving). Forget knives and forks just pick them up and eat them caveman style.

Test practice 3

3

I just don't agree with the way that animals are killed or the way they are kept. So I thought, 'No, I can't put up with this any more – I'll just eat vegetables.' I mean I'd rather go out with a gun and kill a pigeon myself, take it home, pluck it, skin it, cook it. I'd rather do that than go to a supermarket and buy this dead bird that's on display – you know: 'Oh that one's not big enough. I don't want that one ... I'll have this one that hasn't got so much fat on it.'

Section C

This section of the paper is a test of writing. You will be assessed on:

◆ *your ideas and the way you organize and express them*

◆ *your ability to write clearly, using paragraphs and accurate grammar, spelling and punctuation.*

Read the texts on pages 156–7. The first is an extract from a travel guide; the second is an extract from a crime novel.

*When you have read the texts choose **ONE** of the following:*

EITHER:

a The story extract ends in the middle of a sentence.

Write a continuation of the story.

You should use the information from text 1.

OR

b Read text 1 carefully.

Write a short story about some first-time visitors to this place and their reactions to it.

OR

c Choose an interesting place that you know well.

Write an entry for a travel guide in which you describe the attractions and drawbacks of the place you have chosen.

Test practice 4

1

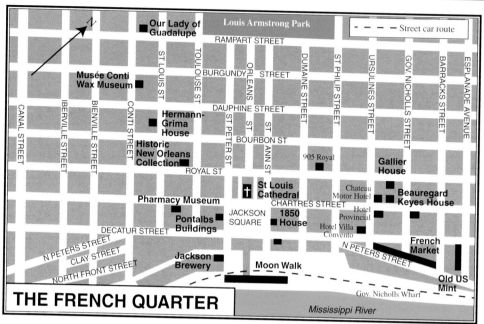

THE FRENCH QUARTER

The French Quarter

Breathtakingly beautiful, depressingly tacky, the **French Quarter** is the heart of New Orleans. Each block, with its overhanging lacy ironwork balconies, crumbling pastel stucco walls, wooden shutters and high-walled cobbled courtyards, smacks of history and legend. Official tours are useful for orientation, but it's most fun simply to wander – and you'll need a couple of days at least to do it justice, absorbing the jumble of sounds, people, sights and smells. Early morning, in the pearly light from the river, is a good time to explore, as sleepy locals wake themselves up with strong coffee in the neighborhood cafés, shops crank open their shutters and all-night revelers stumble home.

Around Bourbon Street

Bourbon Street is the most famous – and most tawdry – pocket of the city.

Lined with strip joints, neon bars and souvenir shops, with a couple of great bars, it is in fact one of the least appealing streets of the Quarter. Luckily, it doesn't take much to escape the place; cut into any of its cross streets to rediscover peace and sanity. Half a block north at 820 St Louis St, the restored 1831 **Hermann-Grima House** *(Mon–Sat 10 a.m.–3.30 p.m.; $5;* ☎ *504/525-5661)* illustrates the lifestyle of middle-class Creoles in the city's golden age. Cooking demonstrations are held in the kitchen every Thursday from October to May. …

The church of **Our Lady of Guadalupe** at 411 N Rampart St, on the corner of Conti Street, is notable for its statue of 'Saint Expedite', mysteriously delivered here, so the legend goes, in a crate simply stamped *expedite* [Fast Delivery].

2

The neon lights on Bourbon looked like green and purple smoke in the rain. The Negro street dancers, with their heavy metal clip-on taps that clattered like horseshoes on the sidewalk, were not out tonight, and the few tourists were mostly family people who walked close against the buildings, from one souvenir shop to the next, and did not stop at the open doors of the strip joints where **spielers** in straw boaters and candy-striped vests were having a hard time bringing in the trade.

I stood against a building on the opposite corner from Smiling Jack's and watched Jerry through the door for a half hour. He wore his **fedora** and an apron over an open-necked sports shirt that was covered with small whiskey bottles. Against the glow of stage lights on the **burlesque** stage behind him, the angular profile of his face looked as though it were snipped out of tin.

The weight of the .45 was heavy in my raincoat pocket. I had a permit to carry it, but I never had occasion to, and actually I had fired it only once since leaving the department, and that was at an alligator who attacked a child on the **bayou**. But I had used it as a police officer when the bodyguard of New Orleans's number-one pimp and drug dealer threw down on my partner and me. It had kicked in my hand like a jackhammer, as though it had a life of its own; when I had stopped shooting into the back of the Cadillac, my ears were roaring with a sound like the sea, my face was stiff with the smell of the cordite, and later my dreams would be peopled by two men whose bodies danced disjointedly in a red haze.

This district had been my turf for fourteen years, first as a patrolman, then as a sergeant in robbery investigation, and finally as a lieutenant in homicide. In that time I got to see them all …

spielers	employees who go out on the the sidewalk (pavement) and try to persuade passers-by to come in
fedora	a broad-brimmed felt hat, often black
burlesque	bawdy comedy show, often with strip-tease
bayou	a slow-flowing stream leading through swampy land to a bigger river